Congrat... YO-CAF-297

You have just purchased Lillian & Jennifer Too's Fortune and Feng Shui personalized horoscope book for 2010!

You've made a great investment in your future and you'll love the specialized insights on what to expect in terms of love, business, wealth and career in 2010!

But wait! Don't' Stop Here... There's More!

Now you can discover other powerful feng shui secrets from Lillian Too that go hand-in-hand with the valuable information you will find in this book.

And it's ABSOLUTELY FREE!

LILLIAN TOO's
NEW Online Weekly Ezine FREE!

You've taken the first step by purchasing this book. Now expand your wealth, luck and knowledge and sign up immediately! Just go to www.lilliantoomandalaezine.com and register today!

It's EASY! It's FREE! It's FRESH & NEW!

Don't Miss Out! Be one of the first to register at
www.lilliantoomandalaezine.com

**Lillian's NEW Online FREE Weekly Ezine is only available to those who register online at
www.lilliantoomandalaezine.com**

LILLIAN TOO & JENNIFER TOO

FORTUNE & FENG SHUI

TiGer

2010

Fortune & Feng Shui 2010 TIGER
by Lillian Too and Jennifer Too
© 2010 Konsep Lagenda Sdn Bhd

Text © 2010 Lillian Too and Jennifer Too
Design and illustrations © Konsep Lagenda Sdn Bhd

The moral right of the authors to be identified as authors of this book
has been asserted.

Published by KONSEP LAGENDA SDN BHD (223 855)
No 11A, Lorong Taman Pantai 7, Pantai Hills
59100 Kuala Lumpur Malaysia

For more Konsep books, go to www.konsepbooks.com
or www.lillian-too.com
To report errors, please send a note to errors@konsepbooks.com
For general feedback, email feedback@konsepbooks.com

ISBN 978-967-329--028-4
Published in Malaysia, July 2009

for more on all the recommended
feng shui cures, remedies & enhancers for

2010
please log on to

www.wofs.com/2010

and

www.fsmegamall.com

YEARS OF THE TIGER

Birth Year	Western Calendar Dates	Age	Kua Number Males	Kua Number Females
Fire Tiger	13 Feb 1926 to 1 Feb 1927	84	2 West Group	4 East Group
Earth Tiger	31 Jan 1938 to 18 Feb 1939	72	8 West Group	7 West Group
Metal Tiger	17 Feb 1950 to 5 Feb 1951	60	5 West Group	1 East Group
Water Tiger	5 Feb 1962 to 24 Jan 1963	48	2 West Group	4 East Group
Wood Tiger	23 Jan 1974 to 10 Feb 1975	36	8 West Group	7 West Group
Fire Tiger	9 Feb 1986 to 28 Jan 1987	24	5 West Group	1 East Group
Earth Tiger	28 Jan 1998 to 15 Feb 1999	12	2 West Group	4 East Group

You are an TIGER born if your birthday falls between the above dates

Contents

OVERVIEW OF THE TIGER YEAR 2010

The Golden Tiger Year of 2010 reflects the character of the Tiger – an aggressive, fierce and tough year that is also resilient and with hidden good fortune possibilities. There are obstacles ahead due to clashing elements, and the aggressive nature of the Tiger Year makes things worse. We face a scenario lacking in good signs; several traditional indicators suggest a challenging and difficult year. For many animal signs, 2010 is a time of tough choices and hard circumstances. For the Tiger born, your own Tiger year brings some dangers to your Life Force, but the year strengthens your inner chi strength. As long as you can stay healthy, the year should bring some exciting opportunities.

Tiger Years bring out the best in many people. Forced to overcome strenuous situations, many rise to the challenge and as a result, those who think positive, act decisively and bring strategic inputs into their work see their efforts bearing fruit. For the Tiger born, the year promises success in the third quarter. There is not much in the way of financial rewards and the advice is for you to focus on maintaining good health and staying strong.

The Golden Tiger Year does not bring smooth sailing; but if you can stay resilient, you can successfully transform the year's problems into opportunities. It is vital not to get mentally defeated by the energy and feng shui afflictions of the year. The Tiger must understand that it is better to recognize the essence of afflictions and then subdue them. Cures and remedies should be effectively applied. The coming twelve months from February 4th 2010 to February 4th 2011 will test the most resilient of professionals, and the most positive amongst us. The Year of the Ox just passed has been relatively stable but nevertheless fragile. The year of the Tiger is less stable, and conditions for work and business will be more difficult.

This is a year when the elements clash directly – the **Metal** of the year's heavenly stem destroys the Tiger's intrinsic **Wood**. Superficially, this is not a good sign. Yet metal, when used with skill and under special circumstances can transform Wood into something of great value. So even as Metal destroys Wood, it can transform Wood into an object of value. This is the hidden worth which all should strive to capture.

With the elements of the year clashing, hostilities can get uglier; competition nastier and the environment itself more hostile. Heaven and Earth energy are not in sync. It is left to mankind - men and women ourselves - to use our creativity and prowess to rise to the challenges and emerge triumphant.

Natural luck is in short supply. But this does not mean we cannot create our own luck! The year's outlook simply manifest the way the elements of the year have arranged themselves – as revealed in the Paht Chee chart, and in the Flying Star feng shui charts of 2010. These charts have proved accurate in past years and are worth analyzing.

Note however that while the elements of the year influence the way luck manifests on a macro level, it is at the micro levels that an individual's luck is determined; and your elements at the micro level can be enhanced or subdued, can be transformed and made better. Here is where understanding astrological indications and feng shui can be so helpful. There are ways to overcome negative energies caused by a clash of elements brought by missing elements, made worse by visiting "stars" of the 24 mountains or affected by elements that are hidden in the paht chee chart of the year. The "afflictions" we have to confront in the Year of the Tiger, or in any year, can all be remedied.

Remedial Actions

We can create elements that are missing; replenish those that are in short supply; subdue misfortune stars and strongly activate the positive stars that bring good fortune to any home. This is the feng shui aspect of corrective work that can be done to improve the prosperity potential of your home.

The luck of individuals can also be improved by using element astrology and this is laid out in detail in the section on Annual Element Horoscopes which explain how the different elements of the Tiger Year affects you based on your animal sign of the Tiger and your stem element. This year we also offer suggested remedies. You can examine the pluses and minuses of your horoscopes to improve your luck for the year. You can use our suggestions and take steps to minimize whatever horoscope obstacles afflict your sign.

Determine the elements that are missing or weak in your birth horoscope. Note what element requires replenishment; take note of particular afflictions that can cause you the most problem. Then subdue them. Your animal sign scenario and outlook changes from year to year, so it is important to update.

Four Pillars Ruling the Year

PAHT CHEE CHART 2010 - YEAR OF THE GOLDEN TIGER			
HOUR	**DAY**	**MONTH**	**YEAR**
HEAVENLY STEM 己 YIN EARTH	HEAVENLY STEM 乙 YIN WOOD	HEAVENLY STEM 戊 YANG EARTH	HEAVENLY STEM 庚 YANG METAL
EARTHLY BRANCH 乙 卯 RABBIT WOOD	EARTHLY BRANCH 辛 酉 ROOSTER METAL	EARTHLY BRANCH 甲 寅 TIGER WOOD	EARTHLY BRANCH 甲 寅 TIGER WOOD
HIDDEN HEAVENLY STEMS OF THE YEAR			
YIN WOOD	YIN METAL	YANG EARTH YANG WOOD YANG FIRE	YANG EARTH YANG WOOD YANG FIRE
The year is desperately short of WATER			

The year's ruling four pillars chart (illustrated here) shows there is an excess of Wood element, led by the Tiger whose intrinsic element is Yang Wood. Tiger appears twice, in the Year and in the Month Pillars, making its influence and that of the Wood element very strong. Note also that another Yin Wood is brought by the Rabbit. So there are three wood branches in the chart. These are supplemented by yet another wood, i.e. the Yin wood stem of the

Day Pillar, making a total appearance of four Wood elements in the chart.

The intrinsic element of the year is therefore Strong Yin Wood. This excess of the Wood element suggests a year fraught with competitive pressures, when even friends can become devious in the interests of surviving through a tough time.

But the Wood element will get depleted. Two Earth elements symbolically distract Wood, and two Metal elements symbolically destroy Wood. This would have been fine and even auspicious if the Wood element was being renewed by the presence of Water. The chart however is missing Water and missing Fire. The Wood of the year thus signifies dead and dying wood that cannot grow. With crucial elements missing, expansion and productivity is greatly strained this year. The work scenario is tough!

Unbalanced Chart

With two elements missing and with too much Wood, the chart is considered unbalanced. This is not an auspicious sign. The presence of both yin and yang pillars makes up for this imbalance to some extent as neither positive yang nor negative yin energies dominate.

Two Metal in the chart suggests that power and rank come into focus during the year. There is no lack of leadership or mentor luck, and there is both yang as well as yin metal, male and female. Powerful men and women play a big role in the promise of the year's outlook.

Two Earth elements in the chart signify the presence of wealth luck. There is more wealth luck this year than last year. So despite an imbalance of elements in the chart, prosperity luck is present. This means there are opportunities for making money during the year.

> What is needed to actualize wealth luck in 2010 is Water. It is only when the year's Wood element can flourish, grow and bring itself to fruition that money can be made. Wood needs Water, which is missing; WATER must thus be created!

The missing Water is significant. In addition, Fire is also missing. Without Water there can be no growth luck, and without Fire, there is no creativity! In the chart, the Fire element symbolizes ingenuity, intelligence, strategic thinking and mental clarity. Without clear foresight and creativity, the year lacks the spark to get things moving. Those wishing to succeed must generate the Fire element within their living space, or personify this element by wearing the shades of the fire element – red. Only then will you be resourceful enough to forge ahead. What is needed in the Year of the Tiger is vision and imagination. If you can think of original ways of moving ahead in your career or in your work, you will benefit greatly.

Hidden Elements

Since the year suffers from missing elements, we next examine if there are any hidden elements in the chart. Usually, earthly branches always have hidden heavenly stems and in 2010, the three animals of the year; i.e. the Tiger, the Rooster and the Rabbit do bring additional elements that supplement the year's luck further. The Tiger hides yang Earth, yang Wood and Yang Fire in the chart, and since Tiger appears twice in the chart, there are two hidden Yang Fire.

This suggests hidden creativity, resourcefulness and ingenuity, as a result of which the year benefits. This is a good sign. And since Fire exhausts Wood, its hidden presence will also subdue competitive pressures. However, there is no sign of hidden Water! This serious lack of water means that although the essence of the year is Strong Wood, missing Water suggests rotting and depleting wood. It is hard to accumulate asset wealth in 2010. Those of you who create a powerful water feature in your work or living space are certain to benefit. Water is what brings excellent feng shui to the year 2010!

Crouching Tiger Hidden Dragon

A significant observation of the 2010 paht chee chart is the presence of the Rabbit which belongs to the Wood element, same as the Tiger. The two animals are symbols of Spring, and when combined with the Dragon, a trinity of animal signs get created that produce a very strong seasonal combination of Spring. These three animals rule the East and their combined strength is enormously empowering, especially as their presence is conducive to creating auspicious new beginnings!

The good news is that the Crouching Tiger can cause the Hidden Dragon to surface. This is the source of the well known descriptive phrase "Hidden Dragon, Crouching Tiger" made so famous some years ago by the Ang Lee directed movie of the same name. And since the Month Pillar of the year's chart has Yang Earth, this is the ingredient required for the Dragon to rise from the ground and to fly magnificently into the skies. If this energy can be simulated, the Dragon creates the precious auspicious breath that brings good luck. It is thus significant that there is also the presence of the Rooster in the chart, as the Rooster is

the Dragon's secret friend! The Rooster symbolizes the
Phoenix enticing the Dragon to make an appearance!

Essential water
in the East

*The paht chee chart of the year has the ingredients required
to generate the auspicious presence of the Dragon! It is thus
extremely auspicious to invite the Dragon image into your
home in 2010.*

The Dragon is the celestial creature that will
bring great good fortune to the year 2010.
Place a water feature which has the images of
the crouching Tiger, the hidden Dragon and
the Rabbit in the East sector of the home.

In 2010, this direction is visited by the celestial
heavenly star of 6 which brings good fortune. Placing

Water in the East not only activates the luck of a good Spring, it also makes up for the lack of a *lap chun* caused by the lunar year starting late. The key to creating good energy for 2010 is thus a Dragon/Tiger/Rabbit water feature in the East!

The wearing of any kind of precious or semi-precious earth stone or of any kind of Dragon jewellery is especially meaningful in 2010. The stone signifies Earth which brings wealth luck, while the Dragon activates the luck of new beginnings, transforming the year's Tiger energy to work powerfully in your favor. The Dragon keeps the mighty fierce Tiger under control! This is not necessarily bad for the Tiger born. Keeping its ferocious and powerful energy under control brings out the best in the Tiger born!

Auspicious & Dangerous Stars

In 2010, two potentially auspicious stars and two potentially dangerous stars make an appearance. Both the stars are powerful in their beneficial and malefic influences respectively. The two lucky stars bring good fortune. They impact different animal signs differently and in varying degrees, but they are generally beneficial.

1. Mentor Star

In Chinese astrology, much is made of "mentor" luck, which in the old days was a major factor bringing career success. This suggests there is patronage luck available to the younger generation. If you are working towards clear cut career goals, you can attract mentor luck. You can find powerful benefactors, and in 2010, success comes from "who you know rather than what you know." This star is also referred to as the Heavenly Virtue Star. With its presence in the chart of the year, it indicates help comes from powerful people. To activate for this star to manifest successfully for you, use the **Double Six Big Smooth Amulet**, an amulet comprising six large coins laid out in a row.

2. Star of Prospects

This favorable star brings a special energy that rewards determination and staying power. Those who have a passion for success will benefit from its presence. There is nothing that cannot be achieved for those prepared to work hard. Here we see ambition playing a big role in making the best of what the year brings. To activate this star in your favor, make sure you have a Rabbit image in the water features placed in your home.

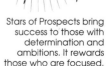

Stars of Prospects bring success to those with determination and ambitions. It rewards those who are focused.

3. Aggressive Sword Star

This star is brought by the Tiger and there being two Tigers, it suggests that the Aggressive Sword's negative effects comes with a double whammy. This star brings fierce, ruthless and violent chi energy. People will push ahead at the expense of others using fair means or foul. The name of this star is *Yang Ren*, which describes yang essence (as in yin or yang) sharp blade that inflicts damage. This star has great potential for good or bad influences to materialize during the year, but it is more negative than positive. The excess Wood in the year's chart makes things worse.

To be protected from falling victim to this star's aggressive influence, you must wear the **Double Ring Talisman**. Also excellent for overcoming the ferocity of the Aggressive Sword Star are the **Trinity Ring** and pendants signifying heaven, earth and mankind chi. These come with powerful mantras of the Lotus family of Buddhas – Amitabha, Chenrezig and

Wear the Trinity Ring with mantra to protect yourself against the Star of Aggressive Sword. This Trinity Ring also signifies the trinity of *tien ti ren* - which is very auspicious.

Manjushuri. Finally, a third remedy is the **Fire Magic Wheel** for those who may be especially badly hit by the year's fierce Tiger energy. If you find yourself falling ill a lot or being hit by big doses of bad luck and disappointments, any one of these amulets are powerful ways to repel the bad luck.

4. Flower of Romance Star (External)

This is sometimes confused with the *peach blossom star* because it addresses the destiny of love. When the *flower of romance* is present in any year, it suggests love blossoms easily between people but it is not the kind of love that leads to marriage and family; it indicates instead, the possibility of extramarital affairs bringing stress to happily married couples.

There is a difference between internal romance and external romance, and in the year of the Tiger, it is the latter rather than the former that prevails. So the year will see increased occurrences of infidelity.

In 2010, the Rabbit in the Hour Pillar is the Romance Star of the Tiger, and because Rabbit occurs in the Hour Pillar, it signifies the *external romance star* and this makes all marriages vulnerable.

Things are made worse by the Rooster in the Day Pillar, as Rooster clashes with Rabbit. This causes misunderstandings, although for the most part, infidelity in 2010 will not lead to divorce.

Tiger born people wanting to protect their marriage from the Star of External Flower of Romance must place the image of the Rooster either in the East of your room, or in your own direction of NE3! The most vulnerable months for you are March and also December as these are the months when there could be infidelity temptations. Wearing amethysts also helps to prevent infidelity.

Year's Feng Shui Chart

The destiny luck of the year is also influenced by the year's feng shui chart, which reveals lucky and unlucky sectors of buildings, houses and apartments. The chart comprises a three by three sector grid of numbers that reveal the luck distribution of the year. 2010's chart is explained in detail in Part 4 of this book.

In addition, the fortune-bringing stars of the 24 mountains also affect the luck of the different sectors of your living space. The Fortune Stars add important nuances to what is revealed in the annual chart and their combined influences also affect the luck of each individual animal sign. There are 108 different Fortune

Stars, but only a handful fly into each of the 24 mountain directions in any year. These bring auspicious or harmful influences, but they vary in strength and type each year.

The 24 Mountain Stars affect houses and animal signs equally. Some stars bring good luck, some bring misfortune, while others bring protection. When your sign is negatively afflicted and your vitality gets weakened, you need to wear specific protective Taoist charms. When your energy is heightened, the stars help you to manifest whatever good fortune comes your way. These are explained in detail for your sign in Part 5 of the book.

Monthly Readings for the Whole Year

> For the Tiger, do note that the Hsia calendar months of Dog (October), Horse (June) and Boar (November) will be months when allies and friends make the energies favorable.

This book contains month to month readings of your luck to highlight the different chi energy of each month. They reveal significant high and low points of each month. The idea is to be alerted auspicious as well as unlucky months.

Nothing works better than to be prepared for sudden reversals of fortune, and in knowing when a particular misfortune can happen. When forewarned you have enough time to put remedies into place and to wear cures to suppress the affliction. This is the best way of avoiding misfortunes! Better to subdue bad luck than to wait for bad things to happen and then regret.

This is what motivates us to carefully research and analyze the Almanacs and source books to bring you accurate monthly readings that are an essential component of these books. Timely warnings are given in the monthly readings on Career, Business, Family, Love and Study luck.

These take account of each month's Lo Shu numbers, element, trigram and paht chee luck pillars. These are usually very accurate not just in identifying your good and bad months; they also offer valuable advice on when to lie low and when to move bravely and confidently forward. It will help you to get your timing right on important decisions and actions.

Our books on the twelve animal signs this year follow our tradition of bringing advice that is specific, focused and timely. The recommendations here are meant to alert you to months when you are vulnerable to illness, accidents or dangers. The good luck months are when significant opportunities come to you. Knowing *when* is certain to give you a competitive edge. This year we have added new dimensions that bring yet greater depth to our recommendations on timing.

Your Feng Shui in 2010

A section is devoted to vital Feng Shui updates to be attended to at the start of each New Year. This explains transformational energy patterns that create new lucky and unlucky sectors in 2010. You can then make all the necessary adjustments to the feng shui of your home and work place.

Remedial cures are always necessary to dissolve bad energy that bring misfortune, accidents, illness and other afflictions. All houses are affected by new energy patterns. You may have enjoyed good feng shui last year, but the pattern of chi will have changed in 2010.

An excellent example is the NE sector of the home which is the home location of the Tiger. Last year this sector was hit by the harmful quarrelsome star 3 but in 2010 another kind of affliction hits you, this time its the illness 2. But the good news is that your Tiger direction this year enjoys the protection of the Tai Sui who is the God of the Year. The Tai Sui is a powerful star and when correctly energized brings opportunities to improve your situation. The only problem is that the Tiger born is also vulnerable to the illness star.

Element therapy is very effective for neutralizing bad energy patterns such as the illness star and for strengthening the good sectors. This year, the good luck star number 8 is in the center of the chart. This development indicates that the year strongly benefits those whose homes have open plan concept that does not 'lock up" this auspicious star number.

If you have a toilet or a store room in the center of the home, this can cause good luck to dissipate or stagnate; but if the center of your home is an open space, the good fortune chi flows seamlessly into the living areas of the home; and then 8 in the center brings extreme good fortune, more so when you install a bright light here.

When the luck of 8 of the center is able to flow to other sectors, it particularly benefits the SW and the NE, as these are locations visited by the afflictive stars 2 and 5, two earth numbers that transform into potential good fortune stars when they connect with the 8 to form the parent string combination of 2/5/8. Such a configuration which suppresses the negative aspect of 2 and 5 is only possible when there are no walls to block the energy of 8 from flowing outwards.

Generating Wealth Luck

This is not going to be an easy year, but there is potential to create wealth. Not the kind of mega quick bucks generated through escalation of capital appreciation; instead, wealth will be made in new areas of creative enterprise. It will also be risky because the Year of the Tiger always holds risks. Riding the Tiger requires courage and nerves of steel!

The world's economy is presently going through a major transformation; we are living through the Age of an Information Revolution where news/technology and ideas are accessible to everyone. New wealth comes less from traditional sectors and more from new creativity, technology, energy sources and ways of packaging. In short, from inventive product and service initiatives.

It is advisable to start the Tiger Year by being defensive. You will benefit from being protected, so make very sure to place cures in all the afflicted sectors of your office and home. It makes sense to subdue the ferocious side of the Tiger. For those with dreams of making money and are prepared to take the risks, you can symbolically "ride the Tiger to activate its wealth enhancing potential" but if you are planning on taking business risks this

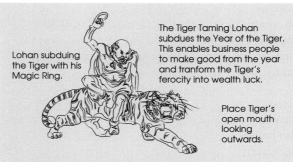

Lohan subduing the Tiger with his Magic Ring.

The Tiger Taming Lohan subdues the Year of the Tiger. This enables business people to make good from the year and tranform the Tiger's ferocity into wealth luck.

Place Tiger's open mouth looking outwards.

year, then you are well advised to enlist the aid of the "Tiger-subduing deities". Most famous of the Taoist deities are the **Tiger-Taming Lohan**, the **Wealth God sitting on a Tiger**, and the **Immortal astride the Tiger**.

Chinese legends contain tales of the wealth-bringing prowess of wise old Tiger, but this can only be unleashed when the wild side of this ferocious beast is adequately tamed! Hence in the Year of the Tiger, it benefits to invite in the three powerful deities who are close to the Tiger into your home. To many Chinese, they are the most powerful of Wealth Gods and their presence in any home or office attracts abundance.

You can also energize the earth element for the center of the house to attract wealth luck and this is because earth energy stands for wealth luck in 2010.

To signify earth, nothing works better than a circular orb rotating in the center of the home to attract wealth luck. So a powerful wealth energizer for the home or any living or work area is to have a **solid rotating crystal ball** in the center.

Those that come with an 8 embedded in gold in the center of the crystal ball are the best, although those who believe strongly in the power of mantras can also place the *Om Mani Padme Hum* rotating crystal ball here.

Last year we designed just such a crystal ball, but we embossed the 21 Tara Praises onto the crystal ball and these brought so much good fortune for us and everyone who used them. Rotating the crystal ball makes it very yang and that is what makes it generate fabulous energy. Shine a light on the crystal to empower it and to make it even more beautiful.

Luck of Elements

Staying lucky requires you to be personally empowered. The aura around you must be radiant and strong, not stagnant and weary. Hence being properly energized, being healthy and staying astrologically strong are the three ingredients of attaining success luck in any year.

What is important is to know exactly how your own personal elements interact with the elements of the year in five important categories. Each of you, depending on your year of birth are born with different elements that affect the strength and quality of your **Life Force** energy; your **Inner Essence**; your **Success Potential**, the stability of your **Financial Luck** and the state of your **Health Luck**.

Your horoscope reveals the ruling elements that govern each of the five categories of luck, and how they interact with the five luck elements of the year. In 2010, the Life Force of the year is Wood, and its Spirit Essence is Water. Hence you can see that it is Water that strengthens Wood… it is the Spirit Essence that strengthens the Life Force of the year.

The year's Health Luck is governed also by Wood while both the year's financial and success potential are governed by Metal. To find out how each person's birth elements interact with the luck elements of the year, we need to analyze how each person's element interacts with 2010's elements. This provides important information that enables you to enhance your potential enormously.

The analysis is based on your year of birth your heavenly stem and your earthly branch. Once you know how strong or how weak your horoscope elements are in 2010, you can easily dress, live and arrange your living space accordingly. This is discussed in detail for you in Part One of this book.

Power of Talismans

Protective talismans have the power to ward off misfortunes and each New Year it is incredibly important to know what talismans to wear and place in your home to ward off bad luck. In the Tiger year, its imbalance of energy must be attended to if you want the year to be smooth for you. Protective amulets possess added potency when made correctly.

Usually, circular discs and squares make excellent shapes for amulets. The built in metal element energy of amulets made of steel or brass and with gold finish have great power to suppress illness and misfortunes brought by the year's afflictive star energies.

The Chinese Almanac is an excellent source of talisman designs and good almanacs provide detailed images with invocations and explanations. These are older, rare editions which we have painstakingly compiled over the years as reference materials to ensure the amulets made comply with vital specifications.

We have discovered that Tibetan-style talismans are very potent; these incorporate Sanskrit and Tibetan mantras which are really extremely powerful. In the old days, Tibetan protection amulets were created by monasteries or very high lamas. These usually comprised mantras and images written onto paper and then folded to resemble mystical knots.

Traditional talismans are often covered by five colored cloth and tied with five colored string which signify the five elements. Modern day amulets maintain the essence of the talismans but their quality of production is much better. In terms of potency they are equally powerful, if not more so, as modern technology has made it possible to have incredible number of mantras to be inserted into the amulets!

Tiger Year Talismans

Here are some important amulets (and a couple with rituals) required for the coming year.

Double 6 Big Smooth Coins

This is a powerful enhancing good luck charm suitable for the year 2010 as it invokes the Star of Powerful Mentors. The six large coins made of metal with gold finish ensure everything goes smoothly for you. Having it in your possession will bring you influential help of someone powerful when you need it. Those in leadership or managerial positions benefit from carrying it. The 48 year old Water Tiger will particularly benefit and get ahead in their professional careers when they place this enhancing amulet on their desks.

The Double Circle Amulet

This wards off seriously troublesome chi energy brought by the combination of five yellow with the illness star afflictions. Wearing it as a pendant or hanging it in your animal sign direction is an effective way of overcoming the troublesome months where the configuration of star numbers bring combined danger of illness and misfortunes.

The Tai Sui Amulet

This invokes the protection and goodwill of the Tai Sui who this year is once again a military general. This amulet carries a special Taoist invocation and the image of a pair of Pi Yao. The Tiger born is supported by the Tai Sui, nevertheless it is a good idea to carry the amulet anyway and this is because the amulet works by appeasing the Tai Sui.

For the Tiger born, it is even more important and beneficial to appease the Tai Sui!

Tai Sui Amulet.

5 Element Ringing Bell

The sound of metal hitting against metal creates the chi energy that can dissolve the power of the five yellow which in 2010 hurts the matriarch in all families. It is important not only to have this bell displayed in the SW corners of the home, but ringing the bell at least once a week magnifies its strength many times over. Walk round each of your rooms in an anti-clockwise direction three times, all the while ringing the bell. This is an energy cleansing ritual which is safe and effective to use. It was not easy finding the kind of bells that produce the melodious sounds preferred for these bell amulets. But when you ring the bell you are instantly dissolving bad energy build up in your space. Do this ritual in rooms that are important to you. Tiger born people should undertake the bell ringing ritual on Fridays of the week.

Excellent for NW & West and absolutely essential in the SW. This is an excellent cure for overcoming the *wu wang,* which in 2010 hurts the matriarch. Mantras embossed on the bell empowers it.

5-ELEMENT
RINGING BELL

The Magic Fire Wheel Talisman

This is the Dharmachakra eight-spoked wheel surrounded by a circle of fire, indicating fire and gold energy. Inscribed in the circle is a very powerful mantra for subduing quarrelsome energy directed towards you. This talisman can effectively reduce gossip, slander, and office politics and even help you avoid court cases and legal entanglements. If you can consecrate these magic fire wheels, they are also effective protection against spirit harm.

Blue Water in a Globe

This Water element talisman is a potent way of making up for the lack of water in this year. Carrying this amulet everywhere you go symbolically brings growth luck. Water feeds the Wood energy of the year and this amulet is especially suitable for those born in the year of the Tiger whose intrinsic element is Wood, which benefits from Water. Having it is sure to add strength to your life force as well as supplement your chi strength, making it easier for good fortune to manifest for you.

A drop of water is like an ocean. Water element brings prosperity in 2010.

Good Income Luck Talisman

Fashioned as a wealth vase, this amulet contains the Taoist wealth fu written on one side, with coins and ingots on the other side. This talisman is excellent to wear to protect against being laid off, losing one's source of income or to ensure that good business luck continues.

Precious Ring Talisman

This powerful ring talisman is said to possess magical powers. It is the main tool of the Tiger taming Arhat who was a Brahmin named Pindola. Made of steel and plated with real gold, inside, the ring can be inserted powerful Dharmakaya mantras. The ring can be hung in the NE corner of your living room or office or you can carry it with you as a bag hanging. The precious ring talisman is one of the most powerful ways of subduing the negative energy of a Tiger Year.

Precious Ring Talisman for taming the Tiger in 2010. Ring is hollow inside, where precious Dharmakaya mantras can be inserted.

Part 1
Outlook for
the Year 2010

- Earth Tiger – 12 & 72 years
- Metal Tiger – 60 years
- Water Tiger – 48 years
- Wood Tiger – 36 years
- Fire Tiger – 24 years

The Tiger born person is subject to competitive pressures, intense politicking and can get drawn into intrigues that will take their toll on you. At a gross level, the main affliction causing problems for the Tiger this year is the illness star 2 which makes you prone to illness. Be wary of epidemics and cut down on your travel. At a subtle level, Tiger must watch the company it keeps. There is danger of getting involved in something dangerous.

The luck of different Tigers in 2010 is not even; neither is it balanced or harmonious. Some of you will do better than the others. With the presence of two Tigers in the paht chee chart of the year, only one emerges the winner. Thus the year, being short of Water and Fire favors the Water Tiger and the Fire Tiger the most. Both these Tigers enjoy splendid health and wealth luck, with the 48 year old Water Tiger registering outstanding prosperity fortune.

In terms of success potential, all Tigers are in for some disappointment, so it is a year to sit tight and keep low-key. Do not roar or get involved in a fight. It may be your year, but other animals fare better than you in 2010.

The Tiger Personality in 2010

The Chinese do not like their daughters to be born into the Year of the Tiger, but that was in the old days when superstition associated the Tiger person with fierce energies. The sign of the Tiger carries several magnificent connotations in Chinese horoscope lore, many linked to its bravery. Merely being born in a Tiger Year is believed to bring you protection against thieves, cheats and evil-minded people. Tigers are viewed as walking amulets! So you have built-in safeguards and protection!

No wonder then that Tigers are seemingly fearless and courageous.

These days, of course, we all know that the Tiger is like a pussycat with an inner core of kindness that is hidden beneath its amazing survival instincts. See beyond the ferocity of Tiger's eyes and you will see a brave and self-assured fighter who can be impulsive and who does not fully appreciate the full force of its own power. These traits are very much in evidence in 2010 when all eyes are on it, in a year when it is not feeling strong, and when it is not at its best physically or mentally.

> In 2010, the Tiger can succumb to illness and then people will see the Tiger as being less ferocious than its reputation suggests.

The charming thing about the Tiger, irrespective if it is weak or strong, is its deprecating sense of humor, which in a year that does not go smoothly, will surface, thus taking the sting off personal disappointments and bad luck. Most of you have to put up with frustrations and setbacks this year. Some even have to stare failure in the face.

Only the 24 year old Fire Tigers and 48 year old Water Tigers will enjoy success and money good fortune this year. Other Tigers feel the brunt of obstacles that slow things down for you. But Tigers are hardy and tough individuals that never lose their sense of confidence and inner strength.

Courage does not desert the Tiger and in 2010, if nothing else, then this – your belief in yourself - this alone will help you transcend whatever setbacks come your way and help you emerge from 2010 brighter and stronger.

The Tiger's inner confidence is what creates the air of optimism that keeps them on the career ladder. Act true to character and rise above whatever temporary disappointments come your way and the year will soon pass. For lucky Tigers however, your vitality and optimism make you soar effortlessly above many others.

LADY TIGER

BIRTH YEAR	TYPE OF TIGER LADY	LO SHU AT BIRTH	AGE	LUCK OUTLOOK IN 2010
1938	Earth Tiger Lady	8	72	Feeling weak but mentally OK
1950	Metal Tiger Lady	5	60	Disappointments all the way
1962	Water Tiger Lady	2	48	Excellent health & wealth luck
1974	Wood Tiger Lady	8	36	Hindrances cause setbacks
1986	Fire Tiger Lady	5	24	Excellent wealth & health luck
1998	Earth Tiger Girl	2	12	Setbacks but still confident

This is a year of disappointments for some of you. It is also a year when getting sick is easy. Luckily for Fire and Water Tiger females, the young 24 year old just embarking on a career and the veteran 48 year old Tiger lady who is in her prime, the year brings magnificent money luck and also good health. For you two Tigers, the year is exhausting but there are compensations. But for the others, success and money are equally elusive. Energy levels are depleted, so this is not a time to play nice, give up or surrender. This is a year when female Tigers benefit from letting their assertive nature emerge. You need strength to cope with the setbacks that come at you unexpectedly and frequently.

Tiger personalities rarely admit defeat, so when misfortune rears its ugly head, the stronger of their kind tend to become more assertive. It is a good thing that Tiger people are more confident than most, since this belief in their own invincibility will help them through 2010. The Tiger lady will lift her head a couple of inches higher to overcome whatever obstacles surface. For Earth, Metal and Wood Tiger women, to survive in the face of a thousand things going wrong requires them to stay self-assured and unwavering.

The Tiger female has to deal with illness brought by the number 2 star and also by the conflicting elements of the year. But she loses none of her charisma or sex appeal. She might be distracted and weak, but she is still a femme fatale! Tiger women cannot help being ferociously exciting creatures, unshackled by rules and fiercely independent always.

The passionate dimension of their personality is always present. It is no different in 2010 although there could be some dimming of exuberance. But for those amongst you who have success luck, you can grab the mantle and make this truly your year!

GENTLEMAN TIGER

BIRTH YEAR	TYPE OF TIGER MAN	LO SHU AT BIRTH	AGE	LUCK OUTLOOK IN 2010
1938	Earth Tiger Man	8	72	Mentally strong but health woes
1950	Metal Tiger Man	5	60	Setbacks bring ill health
1962	Water Tiger Man	2	48	Financially strong & healthy too
1974	Wood Tiger Man	8	36	Stagnating on the career ladder
1986	Fire Tiger Man	5	24	Very healthy & good money luck
1998	Earth Tiger Boy	2	12	Staying steady despite setbacks

For the Earth, Metal and Wood Tiger guy, 2010 looks like it's going to be really unpleasant. These Tigers will feel the lack of the Fire and Water elements acutely, and the year's conflicting energies also bring difficulties. Success seems hard to come by and for them, there is neither health nor wealth luck.

These Tigers need to stay low key and keep their heads down. For those in their sixties and seventies, it is probably not too much to ask. But for the 36 year old Wood Tiger male, this really goes against the grain of his Tiger temperament. He is not at his best staying quiet and being forced to tone down his plans and ambitions, but disappointments do force him to rethink.

This Tiger gentleman will seem morose, moody and more difficult than ever. But it is hard to curb the Tiger male's natural fighting instincts for too long. So here the situation will see an inner strength pulling him together and perhaps towards the end of the year, we will see some shining moments for this Wood Tiger. It helps if this Tiger surrounds himself with Water!

Meanwhile, for Tiger males born with Fire and Water in their year of birth, 2010 brings exceptional wealth and health luck. For the 24 year old Fire Tiger, there is wonderful health luck giving it natural protection against the illness star. There is also positive money luck so there are exciting times ahead during the year.

But for the 48 year old Water Tiger there is amazingly good financial luck. Money flows in effortlessly and health luck is also good. For this Tiger guy, the year will be very pleasant indeed. For them both, there is also little success, but the outstanding money luck makes up for this somewhat. This does not however put a dent into their self-assurance.

Personal Luck Horoscope in 2010

This section focuses on the Personal Luck Horoscope of the Tiger in 2010. The horoscope chart of elements for each Tiger person is determined by the heavenly stem element of your year of birth.

The Horoscope Chart shows how the Tiger's ruling luck elements in its year of birth interacts with the luck elements of the year 2010. This interaction reveals 5 important kinds of good fortune luck and the horoscope reveals whether these 5 types of luck is good or bad each year.

When the elements governing the 5 kinds of luck for each animal sign (using its year of birth) interact with the 2010 elements governing the same kinds of luck, this reveals whether the year brings strength or weakness to that type of luck. It is extremely beneficial to examine what kind of luck combination your animal sign's element horoscope brings each year as these change from year to year. Let's look at these 5 types of luck:

First, Your Life Force...

This reveals hidden dangers or threats to your life that can cause premature death or bring severe worries. This can come suddenly and with little warning; death for instance can come to perfectly healthy people through accidents or unexpected natural disaster. In recent years, raging wild fires, widespread floods, earthquakes and other natural disasters have brought havoc suddenly and unexpectedly into people's lives. So looking out for such threats is an important aspect of horoscope consultations.

When the Life Force luck shows a double cross - XX – it is vital to wear some kind of **celestial amulet**. The best form of protection is usually something spiritual, a set of sacred syllables or a talisman that carries powerful holy mantras. A double XX does not necessarily bring death. What it brings is a warning that some kind of danger is imminent.

> The Tiger has a single X against its Life Force in 2010 indicating that it needs some kind of amulet protection. Usually when the wearing of amulets is accompanied by some good deed such as performing animal liberation or donating to some charity, misfortune is believed to be successfully averted.

Threats to the Life Force are usually karmic and these can be assuaged by a specific kind action on your part. Sometimes just extending a helping hand to someone is enough to overcome bad luck!

Those whose Life Force shows a single X must watch what they eat. You must be mindful of your speech also, because what you say can bring an unexpected negative reaction. Be mindful of your interactive behaviour with others. Guard against arrogance and if you should get into a fight or an argument, it is advisable to walk away. Give the victory to those who annoy you! Hard to do but very beneficial if your Life Force is showing either one or two Xs. This will transform any bad luck you may be experiencing. So Tigers must exercise patience and restraint in 2010.

A circle and a cross – OX or XO – suggests some kind of protection is needed because there is a likelihood of a small accident or event happening that could cause a great deal of inconvenience and aggravation. When a double or triple O such as OO or OOO appears in your Life Force, this indicates that you are very strong. Anyone attempting to cause you hurt will find that it all rebounds back to them!

Second, Your Health Luck...

This is a direct barometer of your physical health and if yours is showing a double cross - XX - as felt by the Earth Tiger in 2010, it means that 2010 brings vulnerability to health issues. When health luck is not good, work schedules get upset. Poor health luck always implies food poisoning, and you can catch wind born diseases. Even a single cross - X – suggests some kind of health related aggravation. This assails the Metal Tiger!

It is believed that bad health luck is brought by the winds. An excellent way of overcoming the double or single X in your Health Luck horoscope is to hang a **wu lou** to appease the winds in your animal sign location.

In 2010, the Tiger is afflicted by the Sickness Star 2, so this can add to the bad health luck of the 72 year old Tiger and the 60 year old Tiger. For both of you it benefits to place a **metal wu lou** or place the healing **Antahkarana** symbol as additional remedies.

The double circle - OO – against your Health Luck suggests there are no health aggravations at all for you. This is the 48 year old Water Tiger who will get better in 2010 should you have fallen seriously sick last year. Good health indications suggest a happy state of mind with no mental aggravations.

You have an excellent positive attitude which attracts good fortune. A single circle - O – also signals a welcoming attitude. So the 24 year old Tiger is probably the happiest of all Tigers this year as it has OOOs.

Those whose charts indicate a cross and a circle – XO or OX – such as the Wood Tiger, have less to worry about because the circle overrides the cross, so the year will flow smoothly. However, you should still look after your health, as the Tiger has the Illness Star in their sector this year.

Third, Your Finance Luck...

This part of the Horoscope reveals the strength and stability of your economic situation. It also indicates if you can improve your financial situation during the year i.e. whether you can do better than the previous year.

When a double circle - OO - is placed against this luck in your chart, it means you can gain substantial new wealth in 2010 and when your chart indicates three circles – OOO – it means your wealth luck is even more certain to materialise! Your business will prosper and whatever expansion you are planning is sure to bear fruit. This is the case with the 48 year old Water Tiger. Remember we have said that Water is the element that is most lacking in 2010, so the presence of the Water element as the heavenly stem serves this Tiger well in the prosperity stakes. The 24 year old Fire Tiger also enjoys financial luck in 2010 as it has OO in its chart.

A single circle - O - means the year does not bring much change to your finances and you will enjoy a stable situation. There will be few surprises to make you worry.

An indication of crosses is a negative reading. The more crosses there are, the greater the instability of your financial situation. The double cross – XX – indicates ups and downs in your money luck. Business suddenly takes a downturn and profits can get hit by declines. Bad financial luck indications must be countered; and you can do this by making some kind of charitable contribution to ease somebody's financial burden. Generosity is the best antidote to lack of financial good fortune.

Buddhists recommend making offerings to the **White Dzambhala Wealth Deity** who sits on a Dragon, carries the gem spouting mongoose and is attended to by four offering goddesses. This is a powerful antidote to counter unstable money luck. If you even have a single cross - X - against your Finance Luck, you should avoid starting any new business ventures or making investments in property or dabble too much in the stock market. You should be extra careful with your funds. Be conservative. A cross with a circle - OX or XO - indicates a stable situation that is neither very bad nor very good.

Fourth, Your Success Luck...

This category puts attention on how well you will do in your career for the year. It offers accurate indications about prospects for promotion and also tracks your progress at work, in school or in anything that you may be engaged in doing at the moment. It also affects those involved in a competitive situation. The circles and crosses are a measure of how successful you can be.

When three circles - OOO - or two circles - OO - appear, it indicates wonderful recognition and success in all your endeavors; career, work, exams or performance in any competition. When you have three circles, you attain recognition easily as the year's energy favors you. Two circles mean success with some effort.

A single circle – O – is a positive indication of success but you need to refrain from getting big headed. A circle with a cross – OX or XO – suggests support from your direct supervisor or boss but you may not have the support of colleagues and co-workers. Make sure you watch your feng shui at work and do not sit with your back to the door.

When two crosses - XX - appear, they indicate aggravations at work and obstacles that block your success. There will be unexpected setbacks and unhelpful people who will bring out the worst in you.

Be careful if you get a single cross - X - as this means you will suffer from malicious gossip which has a negative influence on how others react to you. Gossip will cause you to stumble and impede your progress. This is the indication for all Tigers in 2010. The nature of challenges facing the Tiger takes this form and you should take note of the remedies that will make things better and more bearable.

If you donate towards repainting or rebuilding any temple or place of worship, you can effectively stop all the slander and negative talk about you. This symbolically washes the dirt away. It is a very powerful antidote to excessive gossip. Try it!

Fifth, Your Spirit Essence...

This last category is in many ways the most important as it reveals insights into your inner resilience and spiritual strength. When your inner essence is strong, it is resistant to spiritual afflictions and you can more easily overcome the lack of other categories of luck.

When it is weak it makes you vulnerable to the negative effect of various wandering spirits. While many of these local spirits are harmless, some can be harmful if you inadvertently anger them; through saying wrong things that get picked up by the winds, by desecrating their "homes" such as cutting down old trees or digging up ant hills without proper ritually seeking permission to do so.

These worldly ghosts can only harm those with low levels of spirit essence indicated by the crosses. But anyone getting hit by them will get sick and doctors cannot find the cause, yet you can get weaker and weaker. This is the most obvious way of knowing you have been afflicted.

A very low spirit essence is indicated by two crosses - XX - although when you get even a single X, you are advised to protect yourself with powerful **mantra amulets**. Wearing anything with mantras or sutras inscribed on them will protect you from the afflictions of low spirit essence.

Sometimes people who dislike you for whatever reason can also use black magic against you. Again, these are usually effective only when your spirit essence is low. So once again it is advisable to be careful when your spirit essence shows a X. The best protection is to wear protective mantra on your body such as a mantra ring or a powerful seed syllable such as **Hum** or **Om**. These offer powerful protection. You can also wear **mantra pendants** and necklaces in gold or the powerful protective **Kalachakra pendant**.

When you encounter a cross and a circle - XO or OX - this suggests anger but it also indicates that you will somehow be shielded from any severe effect. Circles means you have inbuilt protection against spiritual afflictions. A single circle - O - indicates you are blessed and protected from spirit harm. It also means your confidence level is good and this can pull out of a bad luck situation.

Wearing protective mantras on your body can protect you from spirit harm. This Omani pendant is suitable for the Tiger in 2010.

A double or triple circle - OOO - means that there are guardian angels or dakinis (holy beings) watching over you. This is a very auspicious meaning as it reflects that you are fully protected during the year. You are not just spiritually safe but will also be shielded against poor health, loss of wealth and all other obstacles that spoil your success luck.

PERSONAL LUCK
12 & 72 Year Old Earth Tiger

TYPE OF LUCK	ELEMENT AT BIRTH AFFECTING THIS LUCK	ELEMENT IN 2010 AFFECTING THIS LUCK	LUCK RATING
Life Force	Wood	Wood	X
Health Luck	Earth	Wood	XX
Finance Luck	Earth	Metal	OX
Success Luck	Metal	Metal	X
Spirit Essence	Water	Water	O

The Earth Tiger at age 72 looks like it will experience severe health problems in 2010 and the main thing keeping this brave fighter going is the relatively good Spirit Essence holding it together. In what is looking to be an unstable year that is lacking much good news for this Tiger, thankfully its financial situation remains stable. The Tiger ruled by the Earth Element has a single X against its Life Force but a double cross against its Health luck. These indications, when read in conjunction with the illness star affliction do not bode well for this Tiger.

It is advisable to take things easy and not be too active. It is best to stay home.

For the younger 12 year old Tiger of school-going age who shares similar horoscope readings, it is likely that being younger, is more able to withstand the year's sickness energies. Nevertheless, it is still a good idea to turn to feng shui for some heavy duty solutions.

Thus both the young and the old Tiger should wear the **Antahkarana** ring so that this potent healing symbol stays close to their skin at all times. In the home they should place illness chi remedies in the NE sector of the home. The best cure to subdue illness vibes is the **wu lou** but also the **Antahkarana** symbol. Also very helpful if you are a Buddhist is to set up the **Medicine Buddha** altar, as this will be a perfect way of suppressing health woes that can lead to tragic news.

The 12 & 72 year old Tiger can wear the Antahkarana healing symbol as a ring to overcome poor health luck in 2010.

60 Year Old Metal Tiger

TYPE OF LUCK	ELEMENT AT BIRTH AFFECTING THIS LUCK	ELEMENT IN 2010 AFFECTING THIS LUCK	LUCK RATING
Life Force	Wood	Wood	X
Health Luck	Wood	Wood	X
Finance Luck	Metal	Metal	X
Success Luck	Metal	Metal	X
Spirit Essence	Water	Water	0

The 60 year old Metal Tiger has a slightly easier time with a single X against the first four categories of luck. This means that for the year, this Tiger lacks the luck to do very much. There are also serious health concerns and it is necessary to not only be watchful over what you eat and where you go, but in the house it also benefits to install all the cures that can subdue illness vibes.

For this Tiger who is probably already in retirement, the year appears to hold out very little in terms of compensating for the illness indications. However, this Tiger has a wonderful single O in its chi strength and at this age, this alone can be extremely potent in making this old Tiger happy. At the end of the day, it is after all the mind that determines our wellbeing.

As long as you stay upbeat and positive, never losing your belief in yourself and your optimism and enthusiasm for life, the year, while not promising much in terms of goodies, is also not very threatening in terms of other dangers. Apart from health risks that come your way, 2010 holds promise of happiness and you can well surprise yourself with you special inner vitality.

The Metal Tiger is flamboyant and loud by nature and slinking into retirement is not quite its style. So in the midst of anything exciting coming your way, you can continue living life the way you have always lived it – with a swagger and a strut, growling your way through the year!

48 Year Old Water Tiger

TYPE OF LUCK	ELEMENT AT BIRTH AFFECTING THIS LUCK	ELEMENT IN 2010 AFFECTING THIS LUCK	LUCK RATING
Life Force	Wood	Wood	X
Health Luck	Metal	Wood	OO
Finance Luck	Water	Metal	OOO
Success Luck	Metal	Metal	X
Spirit Essence	Water	Water	O

The Water Tiger is in for a very rewarding year financially. You can see from the chart the three OOOs against the category of Financial Luck. This means there is some kind of bonanza luck coming your way in 2010 that is going to make you feel and actually be richer! Your income luck is at its maximum in 2010.

Your health luck also indicates a double OO and this implies some kind of safeguard against the Illness Star Affliction that flies to the Tiger location of NE. Perhaps it is the Water element in your heavenly stem that is bringing you such amazing goodies while some of your Tiger siblings are facing such tough times. Nevertheless, like them, your success luck is at a low level.

Professionally, it is best to stay low key. There is an absence of such luck and this can only mean the year will bring some obstacles that block you from achieving anything substantial.

The best way to ride out the year would be to go with the flow. Enjoy whatever the year brings and refrain from being overly active on the professional or business front. The year is definitely an improvement over the previous year, so you should really be happy about the progress.

Although this is your year, note that the indications are not at all encouraging, so do keep your head down and enjoy the year quietly. Resist all temptations to invest in questionable projects. It is also a good idea to wear or carry a **Wu Lou** amulet to counter the negative health indication in your chart.

The 48 year old Tiger should wear or carry a Wu Lou amulet to counter the poor health indications in its chart.

36 Year Old Wood Tiger

TYPE OF LUCK	ELEMENT AT BIRTH AFFECTING THIS LUCK	ELEMENT IN 2010 AFFECTING THIS LUCK	LUCK RATING
Life Force	Wood	Wood	X
Health Luck	Water	Wood	OX
Finance Luck	Wood	Metal	XX
Success Luck	Metal	Metal	X
Spirit Essence	Water	Water	O

The 36 year old Wood Tiger is facing a tough year when few things go right and almost everything goes wrong. Financially it is a year when you can lose money, so you will need to watch your finances. It is definitely not a year to take risks with your funds as you can easily lose it all. Do not gamble and do not invest too impulsively. Even good deals can go very quickly wrong, and often for no good reason.

From the viewpoint of your work, there is also no success luck on the horizon. Professionally, this looks more like a year when setbacks and disappointments make you wince with frustration. There is gossip and politicking against you and you have to put up with a certain amount of injustice as well.

The best way to cope is to bite your lip and not react. Your health luck is reasonably sound but that does not bring you out of the woods. The Tiger is at risk from the Illness Star affliction, so it is beneficial to make sure you do not succumb to sickness. Always get enough rest and don't expose yourself unneccesarily to viruses. Also try to develop healthy habits this year, or you could quickly find poor health catching up with you.

The good thing is that in spite of all the challenges, the Wood Tiger stays up beat and optimistic. You have great inner strength and fortitude, and this alone can pull you out of a downward spiral. The mind is all powerful and since your inner chi strength is good this year do make the most of it!

Display a Tiger and Dragon Wu Lou in the NE sector to improve health luck this year.

24 Year Old Fire Tiger

TYPE OF LUCK	ELEMENT AT BIRTH AFFECTING THIS LUCK	ELEMENT IN 2010 AFFECTING THIS LUCK	LUCK RATING
Life Force	Wood	Wood	X
Health Luck	Fire	Wood	OOO
Finance Luck	Fire	Metal	OO
Success Luck	Metal	Metal	X
Spirit Essence	Water	Water	O

The young Fire Tiger is certainly in the pink of good health, not surprisingly, seeing how good its financial luck is looking. This young Tiger enjoys excellent health and wealth luck in 2010 which is a definite improvement over last year.

Unlike its Tiger siblings, luck seems to be on its side, so professionally, it is looking good. However, do not expect to have any kind of breakthrough success luck. It is just good to lean on your financial luck this year to propel you into some good experiences. You should also not get discouraged with failure.

The Fire energy brings wonderful vitality to your well being, reflecting the year's paht chee chart which also shows benefits from having the Fire element.

The Fire in this Tiger's heavenly stem brings a certain restlessness to this Tiger, making it want to seek out thrills and spills. Since age is on its side it is likely that the daredevil urges and inner spirit will cause this Tiger to take risks older Tigers would not.

Alas it can be fool hardy, but there is a resilience in this Tiger's chart, so no worries. One should never be against trying things out when one is still young. In any case, an optimistic approach to life is really the Tiger's secret weapon and the source of its strength and power.

Hence in someone young and bursting with energetic enthusiasm, it is a good idea if you find something to do that you are passionate about. This is sure to unlock your natural brilliance and bring you some real satisfaction.

Part 2
Tiger Relationships

In Chinese Astrology, your animal sign creates a variety of influences on your life, most significant of which is how it affects the way you interact with the people around you, your partner, your parents, children, siblings, relatives and friends.

Knowing the fundamentals of astrological compatibilities can help you make your relationships more harmonious, uplifting and definitely less aggravating. You will understand your reactions to people, why you have a natural affinity with some and an instant aversion to others; why some people just annoy you for no reason and why you easily overlook the faults of some others.

It all boils down to the affinity groupings, the secret friends and ideal soul mate pairings of the Chinese Zodiac! The horoscope compatibility groupings influence how you respond to each of the other eleven signs and explain the special relationships that inherently exist between them.

However, there are annual variations to the level of compatibility amongst animal signs. Everyone's energies, moods, aspirations and tolerance levels change from year to year. People tend to be more or less tolerant, more or less magnanimous or selfish, more distracted or warm depending on how they fare during any year.

When things go smoothly one is better disposed to others and even between two animal signs who are naturally antagonistic, there can still be good affinity, enough for two unlikely animal signs to enjoy one another to the extent of becoming temporary soul mates!

Likewise when one is being challenged by a non-stop set of problems, then the slightest provocation can lead to anger even between zodiac friends and allies. That is when friends can become temporary enemies! A falling out between horoscope allies is not impossible.

Hence compatibility between animal signs takes account of time frames. In this section, we look at how the Tiger person relates to others according to specific compatibility groupings, and also how it interacts with other animal signs in 2010.

Compatibility Groupings

1. Alliance of Allies
2. Paired Soulmates
3. Secret Friends
4. Astrological Enemies
5. Peach Blossom Links
6. Seasonal Trinity

1. Alliance of Allies

There are four affinity groupings of animal signs that make up alliances of allies. Each alliance comprises three animal signs who are natural allies of the Horoscope. The three signs within any alliance have similar outlooks and share similar goals. Their attitudes and thought processes are alike, and their support of and compatibility with each other tends to be instant and natural.

When all three animal signs enjoy good fortune in any year, the alliance becomes strong and powerful that year. When there is a natural alliance within a family unit as amongst siblings, or between spouses and a child, the family tends to be very united. They give strength to one another, and when they prosper, good fortune gets multiplied. Families that have alliances of allies are usually extremely close knit. This is one of the secret indications of good fortune. As an alliance, they become a formidable force.

ALLY GROUPINGS	ANIMALS	CHARACTERISTICS
Competitors	Rat, Dragon, Monkey	Competent, Tough, Resolute
Intellectuals	Ox, Snake, Rooster	Generous, Focused, Resilient
Enthusiastic	Dog, Tiger, Horse	Aggressive, Rebellious, Coy
Diplomatic	Boar, Sheep, Rabbit	Creative, Kind, Emotional

Allies always get along. Any falling out is temporary. They trust, and depend on each other and immediately close ranks should there be an external threat. Good personal feng shui comes from carrying the symbolic image of your horoscope allies, especially when they are going through good years.

The Tiger and its allies as a group will find that it is the Horse who is the strongest in the alliance in

2010, and the Dog is the weakest; so both Tiger and Dog need the support of the very strong Horse. The phenomenon of the alliance of allies is that when the allies operate as a group, they can weather the storms of any challenging year more successfully. Here we are thinking of their astrological strength. Thus when the alliance cooperate with each other and team up, their collective inner energies will become magnified; and for this alliance which has the Tiger as a member, the Tiger Year will make it conducive for them to receive good energies.

If your business associates and you comprise this grouping of Dog, Horse and Tiger, the year will be easier to manage. If there are three of you in a family, or within the same department of a company, the alliance can be activated to benefit every member.

> In this alliance, Horse should be allowed to take the lead in 2010. Although afflicted by the quarrelsome star and hence will have a short fuse, Horse has the energy to pull its allies out of their tendency towards tiredness and exhaustion.

In this respect the Tiger is not as weak as the Dog. It being the Tiger Year, its inner essence is at a level which may not be as high as that of the Horse, but it still has a growl. The only problem is that Tiger is vulnerable to succumbing to illness so it is a good idea to have Horse nearby to borrow its strength. In 2010, Tiger enjoys the support of the Tai Sui Star so there will be hidden support. All the Tiger needs to perform well in 2010 is the Water element and some help from its ally the Horse.

Your Life Force could make you physically weak but your spirit is vigorous and your confidence level is good. This is your year so you can definitely make the most of it! Just make certain that there is always a Water type enhancer near you – being of the Wood element, you will need Water to stay strong.

2. Paired Soulmates

There are six pairs of animal signs that can be described as natural soulmates. One sign will be yin and the other yang. In astrology texts they are described as creating the six Zodiac Houses with each one manifesting its own special niche of compatibility. The pairing creates a powerful bonding on a cosmic level, and a marriage or business union between any two people belonging to the same Zodiac House will definitely have instant rapport with each other.

When people talk about 'falling in love at first sight' it is likely they belong to the same House, and should they marry, there is promise of great happiness for them

Houses of Paired Soulmates

Animals	Yin/Yang	Zodiac House of Creativity	Target Unleashed
Rat	Yang	House of Creativity & Cleverness	The Rat initiates
Ox	Yin		The Ox completes
Tiger	Yang	House of Growth & Development	The Tiger employs force
Rabbit	Yin		The Rabbit uses diplomacy
Dragon	Yang	House of Magic & Sprituality	The Dragon creates magic
Snake	Yin		The Snake creates mystery
Horse	Yang	House of Passion & Sexuality	The Horse embodies male energy
Sheep	Yin		The Sheep is the female energy
Monkey	Yang	House of Career & Commerce	The Monkey creates strategy
Rooster	Yin		The Rooster get things moving
Dog	Yang	House of Domesticity	The Dog works to provide
Boar	Yin		The Boar enjoys what is created

as a family. The soulmates pairing spells happiness in a much more concentrated way than any other kind of zodiac alliance. The yin and yang of the two signs indicates the presence of intrinsic male and female essence that taps into a very special cosmic force.

This combination is also great for those who want to work together professionally – e.g. as business partners in a practice - and between siblings. The mutual strength of each pair is different, as some make better commercial partners than marriage partners. How successful you are as a pair depends on how deeply you bond and how close you allow yourselves to get with one another.

A coming together of yang Tiger with the yin Rabbit creates the *House of Growth & Development*. This is a wonderfully upbeat and exciting alliance as together, these two animal signs really bring out greatness in each other.

As the name of their house suggests, this is a pair who is mindful of the future. They look to growth and development all the time and with them there is never a static time. The Tiger will have exciting plans for the future when there is someone born in the Rabbit year around, so you are good for each other. In 2010 the Rabbit is reasonably active and possessed of inner vitality while the Tiger is also able to match the level of yang energy being generated. So the energy of these two animal signs is pretty much on the same wavelength. You work well together in a commercial partnership and in the Year of the Tiger. Secret opportunities come your way. The challenge is for you both to have the luck to recognize them when they come.

3. Secret Friends

The third set of special relationships in the zodiac groupings creates the bond of a secret friendship under which a very powerful astrological affinity is created.

Pairings of Secret Friends

Rat	Boar	Dog	Dragon	Snake	Horse
Ox	Tiger	Rabbit	Rooster	Monkey	Sheep

Secret friends are exceptionally compatible. This is a vigorous union of two equals and works very well as a married couple. There is love, respect and goodwill between secret friends. Theirs is a bond which once forged will be hard to break; and even when they themselves want to call it quits with each other, still it will be hard for either party to fully walk away. This pair of signs will stick together through thick and thin.

They are fiercely protective of each other and even when they are no longer partners there is still some kind of lingering comradeship between them. But one will dominate and it is usually the animal sign whose heavenly stem element controls the other.

In the pairing of secret friends, Tiger is paired with Boar. There is a very special bond between these two animal signs and it appears like a case of opposites being attracted to each other. They have very different personalities, but they find it easy to enjoy one another's company and to be intensely loyal.

As zodiac soulmates, they naturally gravitate towards one another. A marriage between them has a chance to grow into a very happy family unit indeed. The good thing about these secret friends is that they bring out the best in each other, one inspiring the other to great heights. For Tiger, Boar is the only sign of the zodiac that can make it purr with contentment.

4. Astrological Enemies

According to the principles of the Horoscope, the animal sign that directly confronts yours is your astrological enemy who can rarely help you. For Tiger, the enemy is Monkey, and this being a Tiger Year, needless to say, your enemy is at a disadvantage.

Pairings of Astrological Enemies

Rat	Boar	Dog	Rabbit	Tiger	Ox
Horse	Snake	Dragon	Rooster	Monkey	Sheep

But you too must be careful how you position
yourself in the presence of anyone born in a Monkey
Year.

Your astrological enemy does not necessarily harm
you; but your enemy will also never be of much help
either. The elements of the two clash. Monkey is
intrinsically Metal and Tiger is Wood. This suggests
that their animosity does go very deep.

In a direct clash, Monkey will use its crafty and
ingenious brain while Tiger uses sheer physical
strength! From the viewpoint of the Elements Tiger
must be exceedingly wary of Monkey.

A marriage between these two signs is like a marriage
made in the jungle – survival of the fittest; this is
a pairing that is unlikely to benefit either side and
could even hurt one another. They do not have
sincere or deep feelings for one another. Pairings
between arrows of antagonism are better discouraged
unless there are other indications in their respective

paht chee charts. So Tigers are advised to refrain from getting involved with Monkeys!

As a business partnership, the pairing is also likely to lead to problems, and in the event of a split, the separation can be acrimonious even if they start out as friends. In 2010 any coming together of Tiger and Monkey is super bad! There will be betrayal and quarrels between them.

When two opposite signs have a hostile connection this way and they stay in the same house, they cannot be close; they have completely different sets of friends. If they are siblings, they will not share confidences and will eventually drift apart. If they stay apart, there won't be any direct antagonism, but they are unlikely to have much in common.

5. Peach Blossom Links

Each of the alliance of allies has a special relationship with one of the four primary signs of Horse, Rat, Rooster and Rabbit in that these are the symbolic representations of love and romance for one alliance group of animal signs. In the horoscope, they are referred to as *peach blossom animals* and the presence of their images in the homes of the matching alliance of allies brings peach blossom luck which is associated with love and romance.

The Tiger belongs to the alliance of Dog, Horse and Tiger, and they have the Rabbit as their peach blossom link. So here the peach blossom link reaffirms the Tiger's connection with the Rabbit as they also both belong to the seasonal trinity of Spring.

The Tiger will benefit from associating with anyone born in a Rabbit Year, and will also benefit romantically from placing a painting or image of a Rabbit in the East corner of the house, or in the Tiger direction of NE.

6. Seasonal Trinity

There is another grouping of animal signs which creates the four seasonal trinity combinations that bring exceptional luck of seasonal abundance. To many astrology experts, this is regarded as one of the more powerful combinations of animal signs. When the combination exists within a family made up of either parent or both parents and with one or more children, they will collectively be strong enough to transform the luck indications for the family members that make up the combination for the entire year.

This means that even when the annual indications of the year may not appear favorable, the existence of the seasonal combination of animals is sufficient to transform the luck making it a lot better. The best times will also always be felt by the season indicated by the combination.

It is however necessary for all three animal signs to live together or to be in the same office working in close proximity for this powerful pattern to take effect. For greater impact, it is better feng shui if they are all using the direction associated with the relevant seasons. Thus the seasonal combination of Spring is East, while the seasonal combination of Summer is South.

The Tiger belongs to the seasonal combination of Spring, a combination which is especially significant in its own Year of the Tiger. The combination directs focus onto the Dragon's links with the Tiger, and in 2010, with the Rabbit making its presence felt in the year's paht chee chart, this seasonal combination is automatically activated for those born in the years of these three animal signs. Note that should you, the Tiger, be married to a Dragon, and you have a Rabbit child for instance, the three of you forms the trinity of Spring which is most auspicious this year!

And if you, the Tiger, are married to a Rabbit, then together you will need the Dragon to create a seasonal combination which is of great benefit in this Year of the Tiger – the combination has the potential to bring you abundant luck this year; this combination in effect will make up for the missing lap chun, hence jump starting your luck for the year!

The table below summarises the seasonal trinities of the horoscope.

Seasonal Trinities of the Horoscope

Animal signs	Season	Element	Direction
Dragon, Rabbit, Tiger	Spring	Wood	East
Snake, Horse, Sheep	Summer	Fire	South
Monkey, Rooster, Dog	Autumn	Metal	West
Ox, Rat, Boar	Winter	Water	North

TIGER WITH RAT *(Resentment)*
Tiger Resents Being Taken for Granted

This is an unlikely pair as they have little in common. Fun loving Rat cannot find common ground with serious and dour Tiger, who in its own Year of the Tiger seems rather lacking in the kind of vitality one would normally expect from this sign. Younger Tigers will be perkier than older Tigers but generally, Tigers this year tend to be serious and unsmiling through the year; and also rather vulnerable to physical afflictions.

Tiger's life force lacks vigor but it is important for Rat to understand that behind its sleepy eyes, Tiger is ever alert and stays mindful of everything happening around it. In a Tiger/Rat coupling, Tiger will resent being taken for granted, so Rat should tread carefully and not be over confident or excessively dismissive. You would also be unwise to cheat on Tiger, so any thought of flirting outside the relationship should be kept well under control. In this relationship, Rat is strongly advised to give in to Tiger.

In 2010, Tiger's inner essence is stronger than that of Rat and this suggests that in any kind of tussle, it will be Tiger who will prevail. In terms of their horoscope compatibility, the Rat and Tiger in their twenties have a better time than last year as both have high energy levels; nevertheless, the Fire Tiger exhausts the patience of the Wood Rat. Jealousy and resentment arises from Rat looking elsewhere for love. This is a couple better apart than together; but if you do stay together, Rat should not rile Tiger's temper.

For the 37 year old Water Rat and 35 year old Wood Tiger, the year brings unhappy tensions and a great deal of stress. Rat is likely to want to scurry away from the relationship and start again with someone else. Should there be a break, there is no happy ending. Both sides have to make a special effort to stay together. In this pairing, Tiger is weak, more so than Rat who benefits from financial gains this year. Also, Rat's Water energy puts it at an advantage over Tiger. So if it is the Rat wanting to walk away, it might indeed happen.

For the 50 year old Metal Rat and 47 year old Water Tiger, the story is much happier for the Tiger. Here, Tiger is at an advantage and the year is also one of wonderful financial luck. Rat on the other hand will be the weak link in this relationship so here it is best for Rat to stay submissive and ride along with Tiger.

TIGER WITH OX (*Indifference*)
No Real Interest from Either Side

There are no special ties between these two signs and in the astrological scheme of things, zodiac relationships need some kind of link for any pairing to really work on a long term basis. These are two signs are strong characters, with firm views. They can also be rather stubborn to boot. So it is not surprising that they have little interest in one another, unless they happen to be thrown together by some shared passion, sport or hobby.

And even then, any linking up will soon fizzle out and cannot be anything but temporary. In 2010, both have their own interests.

Ox is particularly listless and not interested. Afflicted by the illness star and feeling the effects of a low energy horoscope chart, Ox cannot be bothered to play the sexy siren (in the case of Lady Ox) or the eager suitor (in the case of guys). In short, they are simply not very interested in romance this year.

In the Year of the Tiger, Ox is definitely not interested in love, marriage or in the Tiger person! If already hitched to a Tiger, they will tolerate each other, but there is little real interest in each other. This is a couple distracted by other things. In any case, physically, they are not at their best, as both are vulnerable to the illness star. This hits the Ox harder than it does the Tiger. The year does not have anything pulling them apart, so these two signs will not see one another as adversaries. Despite it being the Tiger Year, there is no special animosity emanating towards Ox. But they are also not "buddies" in that there will not be any easy camaraderie between them.

> The Tiger and Ox have different personalities and their thought processes are also dissimilar. Ox people are much better focused than Tiger people. One is a domestic animal, the other a creature of the wild! So these are two people with little in common.

In 2010, the Ox and Tiger in their twenties are surprisingly open to the idea of a possible relationship between them. Their heavenly stems are also conducive with Tiger being Fire and the older Ox being Wood, so here, Tiger could find Ox attractive enough to kindle some interest. Any relationship started may not last, but for as long as it does, they should have a good time!

As for the Ox/Tiger pairing in their thirties, the Water Ox has little time for the Wood Tiger, being too busy pursuing career interests or other work-related matters.

TIGER WITH TIGER *(Consistent)*
Never Changing Its Stripes

The Tiger is exceedingly serious in its own year. Dour, listless and lacking in vitality, Tiger can be boringly consistent to its own kind. Tigers can of course be highly but in 2010, Tiger tends to be languid rather than fiery. As a couple, they understand each other only too well. So it will generally be an uneventful year.

> With two Tigers, one must give way to the other, because there cannot be two Tigers on the same mountain. With the pecking order established, life becomes smooth and easy.

There are two kinds of Tigers for whom 2010 holds some excitement. The 48 year old Water Tiger can look forward to a good year and should there be a pair of Water Tigers, life takes on rosier hues with some grand financial developments to look forward to. The other lucky Tiger pairing will be between two 24 year old Fire Tigers whose vigor will exceeds all other Tigers. Good health luck means there is strength to go seeking for adventure and actually finding it. The Fire energy of their heavenly stems interact beautifully with the synchronised elements of the year, bringing vitality in large measure. So for this pair, if they can overcome their negative Life Force rating and look at the world with humor, 2010 could turn out to be more exciting that at first evident.

Tigers tend to be mindful of backgrounds and can be snobbish. This trait usually manifests as insensitivity towards other people. In a Tiger Year, this aspect becomes more pronounced. In 2010, how they get along with their own sign depends a lot on their respective social and educational backgrounds. Tigers are not averse to getting involved in a love relationship, but whether or not they can last as a couple depends on how alike are their lifestyles and backgrounds. Tigers are reluctant to change their stripes, not even for their loved ones. They usually cannot compromise when it comes to marrying down!

The luck of 2010 for the Tiger couple is not great as they have to cope with the illness star and negative rating in their Life Force. However, Water and Fire Tigers should find developments good enough for them to get strongly into the swing of the year. Older Tigers tend to succumb more easily to the illness affliction, so for them, remedies to subdue this bad star must be put in place in their Tiger location.

TIGER WITH RABBIT *(Connected)*
In 2010, Mentally & Spiritually Attuned

These two signs are like mirrors of one another, being perfectly in tune mentally as well as spiritually. The Rabbit and Tiger may look very different, but from an elemental and astrological perspective, they are very compatible. They walk and run to the same rhythm, sharing thought processes that reflect their similiar outlook and attitudes. Mainly this arises from their strong connection to the Season of Spring which highlights renewal and birth, or maybe it is because they are both intrinsically Wood element people, hence are mindful of growth energies and the creativity that is inherent and necessary in everything we do.

Whatever it is, Tiger is always drawn to anyone belonging to the sign of the Rabbit. And in 2010, both Tiger and Rabbit make appearances in the year's paht chee chart. This occurrence indicates excellent signals of auspiciousness for a pairing of Tiger and Rabbit. When Tiger meets Rabbit for the first time, their instant connection suggests some kind of inner intuitive connection. Superficial first impressions do not at first suggest any kind of closeness between them. Scratch deeper however, or leave them alone for a couple of hours, and inner connectivity starts to resonate. So if you Tiger meet up with a Rabbit who catches your interest, invest some time together and soon you will be chatting away like old friends! Once you "discover" each other, you might find yourselves becoming quite inseparable. Here we see the loud and seemingly ferocious Tiger falling for the gentle and soft spoken Rabbit. It does not matter about gender; the attraction will be very obvious and electric! The Tiger and Rabbit also make great business partners as their skills are complementary and their outlooks flow in the same direction. Their methods may not be the same, but as a team, they are very effective.

In 2010, all they need is to find themselves a Dragon to make their perfect partnership complete - perhaps a Dragon image or better yet if they already have a Dragon child it would be great! For as a trinity, they form the seasonal combination of Spring. This makes up for the lack of *lap chun* in 2010. Two sets of pairings - the 48 year old Water Tiger and 47 year old Water Rabbit, as well as the 24 year old Fire Tiger/23 year old Fire Rabbit - are the stars of 2010 and enjoy a spectacular financial bonanza year. Both pairs will experience success luck in 2010 as they successfully create a *House of Growth and Development* for their families.

TIGER WITH DRAGON *(Subdued)*
In 2010, Better to Stay Low Key

2010 is a Tiger Year and as if reflecting the ferocity of its seasonal pal, Dragon suffers from very low Life Force and inner chi essence. This hurts Dragon but does not reduce its attraction for Tiger. In terms of their relative luck quota, both have varying degrees of good and bad in 2010, with Tiger being slightly ahead. But thankfully for these two signs, the season of Spring will shower any Tiger/Dragon pairing with a burst of good fortune if they enlist the aid of the Water element, enabling them to somehow connect at a deeper level. In 2010, these two can seize the moment and start the year with a loud show of solidarity and closeness. All they need to do is make up for the lack of a *lap chun* by turning on a water feature in the East part of their home!

This year, the vitality of Dragon lacks intensity. The luck of Dragon is also lacking, so from the start, you powerful and charismatic people must agree on the power levels in your relationship. The Dragon and Tiger are strong personalities and as a partnership, can transform everything they do into something beneficial. The danger is that they can also consume each other with excessive energy. Fortunately, this is unlikely to happen because in 2010, both Dragon and Tiger are relatively weak. They lack the intensity of other years, but this need not work against them. Sometimes reducing energy can be a good thing and there is much to be said for staying subdued.

When suitably motivated, there is nothing they cannot make happen. In business or in a personal relationship, they traditionally make exciting partners. They have great potential for achieving whatever they aspire to. How good the end result however depends on their individual luck from year to year.

But there can be obstacles to their success. Difficulties arise when the year works against them and when that happens, they are better off staying low key. 2010 is not exactly bad because there are also good months, and certain of their signs have quite spectacular luck indications e.g. the 48 year old Water and 24 year old Fire Tigers and the 58 year old Water Dragon. But both have afflictions to contend with, so on balance, they are better off not taking risks. This year it is better to put ambitious dreams of success on hold. Sometimes it can be beneficial to take things slow. No matter how formidable a team you may be, it is better to stay cool and quiet in 2010.

TIGER WITH SNAKE *(Resentful)*
Jealousy Rears Its Ugly Head

Tiger could find itself feeling confused about its reactions to Snake born people, especially those close to them or with whom they have a relationship. Snakes are going through a great year in 2010, and from Tiger's perspective, they can seem to be doing too well. Tiger cannot suppress feeling competitive or inadequate.

Snake is full of verve and spunk this year, seemingly energized by a new kind of vivacity and joie de vivre. This puts Tiger in the shade, resulting in Tiger feeling insecure. As a couple, they will be forced to confront a sudden big divide developing between them. For Tiger, mistrust of the Snake gets triggered by even the smallest things. Tiger feels vulnerable and this is not good for them. Misunderstandings flare up frequently. It looks like it could be a noisy year for this pair.

Snake usually slides away from conflict, as it is not in its nature to face off any sort of direct confrontation; besides, it is feeling very good this year. Snake is inspired by many things and gets a boost from major new developments in its life. There is also a sense of strength pervading the passing of days for Snake. As a result, very little will upset Snake or cause it to lose its cool, so shaking off Tiger's childish tantrums is not a problem.

Tiger on the other hand will find it hard to subdue feelings of animosity and resentment. Those of you already stuck with one another in a marriage will find that because your energies and outlooks are so unbalanced this year, it might be better giving your relationship a rest. You might even consider walking away altogether! Although Tiger thinks of itself as a powerful sign, it cannot really handle Snake in 2010 who is going through a great year.

Between Tiger and Snake there has always been a lack of trust, so in truth this can never be a good match. Snake will just consume Tiger! Should you decide to split in 2010, be prepared for a hard time. Parting for the Tiger and Snake will not be pleasant and will leave both sides bruised. From Tiger's perspective, the best month to split is in the season of Spring!

TIGER WITH HORSE *(Comforting)*
Like Being in a Warm Place

Tiger feels instinctively safe and happy in the comforting arms of Horse who is its friend and confidante rolled into one. Tiger looks to Horse for comfort and warmth in a year when it is feeling rather weak and battered, and Horse does not disappoint! The reason is that Tiger and Horse are particularly well matched.

> Tiger and Horse are kindred spirits who can laugh together and look at the world through special eyes. They share a sense of adventure that enables them to create their own private world. So they understand each other and feel good about being their real selves with each other. Between them runs a special kind of trust that Tiger cannot easily find with others.

Theirs is more than a physical thing! There is a deep and spiritual connection which takes the way they feel towards one another to a very high place. In 2010, Tiger will automatically gravitate to Horse to be comforted. In fact, for the Tiger looking for a mate, they should really keep their eyes opened for a Horse. In the Year of the Tiger, the Horse is in a very strong place. This is a time when its shoulders can be broad and comforting for the Tiger. This should not come as a surprise because the two signs enjoy a very powerful astrological connection. These two will always find magic together.

Surprisingly, this year it will be Horse that does the chasing. The only dark spot on the horizon for this pair is that while Horse cares deeply for Tiger, in 2010 it is hit by the quarrelsome star 3 and this makes it impatient and intolerant, more so than usual. Happily, Tiger is able to ignore tantrums thrown by Horse. This arises from the deep understanding that exists between them. Communication between them is intuitive. There is tolerance and comforting, so this is a match that can be long lasting and happy.

Note that the Tiger and Horse belong to the alliance that includes the Dog. Together they are the "three hunters" of the Chinese zodiac. They are known for their incredible patience especially when stalking prey. In real life, this applies to their having amazing patience when going through tough times. Tiger and Horse share all the attributes of successful hunters, so they have resilience and courage. With Horse by its side, Tiger will enjoy its own year indeed.

TIGER WITH SHEEP *(Aversion)*
Feeling Bored & Disinterested

Tiger has little or no interest in Sheep in 2010. There is nothing that these two signs have in common that could be the spark for warmer feelings to arise and the year in general is not conducive to them getting together. Sadly, these are two people with so little in common, they just end up finding time spent together to be boring and uninteresting. In fact they might even develop an aversion for one another. Those not already together are not likely to respond to any overtures made by the other.

> In certain years they might feel an odd attraction perhaps brought together by some temporary shared interest, but generally they are quite indifferent to one another. In the Year of the Tiger, there is little that can bring this pair together. The energies of the year works against them as a couple.

To the Tiger person, Sheep will always appear too conservative and old fashioned, lacking excitement usually associated with falling in love or doing something worthwhile together. Tiger feels Sheep lacks passion, not at all the type of person with whom anyone can ignite a passionate love affair with. Needless to say, Sheep harbors the same kinds of feelings and is equally averse to starting anything long term with Tiger. But being more diplomatic, Sheep will simply trot away and never badmouth Tiger. In the eyes of the other therefore, neither will measure up, so it is advisable for them to split rather than waste time with one another.

As siblings they will not be close. Most of the time, Sheep's subtlety will be totally lost on Tiger. One tends to be a creature of the wild, while the other is domesticated and would consider itself much more "civilised". Definitely not good together!

Should these two signs be married, it is likely that Sheep is much younger than Tiger. A match between the 60 year old Tiger would work well with the 31 year old Earth Sheep, or the 48 year old Water Tiger might go for the 19 year old Metal Sheep. This has to do with the elements with Sheep element "producing" Tiger element! However, this is an unlikely scenario because Sheep is not at their best this year. There is the affliction of the *wu wang* which brings troubles and misfortunes. Sheep's horoscope element chart is also very weak, so Sheep is not up to being amiable this year. Faced with any kind of challenge, Sheep prefers to give up and walk away. And this is likely to be the case when it comes to trying to start a relationship with a Tiger person.

TIGER WITH MONKEY *(Antagonistic)*
Unfavorable & Unpleasant

In 2010 these two people have to expect a rough time with each other. They bristle with antagonism just being in the same room and this arises from their energies being in conflict this year. The Wood Tiger views Metal Monkey as the enemy and this being a Metal year, all the more so. Tiger will be at its most threatened and Monkey will be at its most defensive. Oh dear, these two animal signs sure will be on the warpath towards each other.

The Tiger and Monkey are not softies. Neither sign gives way when facing someone they view as an adversary and they definitely view one another this way. In 2010 Tiger is not feeling strong despite it being its year. With some of you, we could even be talking about a wounded Tiger especially the older 60 and 72 year old Tigers. Your health luck is not good so be careful, and try to avoid confronting your zodiac enemy, the Monkey.

In 2010 the Monkey is very strong despite it getting hit by the *wu wang*. Water Monkeys and Fire Monkeys are unbeatable this year, so you do not want to mess with them! The 18 year old Water Monkey is not only confident and cocky this year, but also arrogant and conceited to boot. In short, this young

Monkey is totally insufferable from the viewpoint of the 24 year old Fire Tiger, who as it turns out is enjoying a strong year too – so these two could set the stage for explosive fireworks. Being natural enemies, they might let their differences erupt into something serious.

The Water Tiger enjoys strong health and financial luck and should it pair up with the 42 year old Earth Monkey, it is advisable for Monkey to give way and not fight this Tiger.

Some believe that the Tiger/Monkey match possesses underlying currents of communication and the line between love and hate is a fine one; the theory is that should they bring into their equation two children born Boar and Snake, the family unit forms the rare combination known as the *Four Elements Cross* comprising Fire and Water, Wood and Metal; in such a situation, the family as a unit will have two pairs of secret friends! They will then gain wealth and fame as a family.

TIGER WITH ROOSTER *(Agreeable)*
Competitive But Also Very Cordial

The Cat and the Bird – two signs that can be amiable or deadly depending on the quality of outside forces and energy affecting them. In 2010 Tiger is weak, nursing wounds being afflicted by the illness star. Rooster on the other hand is strong and ready to fly to new heights. Its energy levels are vigorous.

> Against the assured poise of Rooster, Tiger reluctantly concedes and paves the way for an unlikely alliance to be forged to their joint benefit. These two are not enemies but alas are also not friends. Rooster is of the Metal element and Tiger is Wood, so underlying their cordial interface can lurk the seeds of betrayal.

Tiger however is clever and not easily fooled. Rooster could have a hidden agenda and if so, they will need to work through issues that surface. Tiger will insist on it. Unfortunately between them will always be concerns that are related to their respective egos and "face". Pride is important to them and is a big part of their relationship. If there is tension between them it will be because of competitive tendencies intruding into their relationship. This is where danger lies for them. Neither Tiger nor Rooster has a long fuse. They are naturally impatient and unless both work at submerging their natural competitive inclinations, tension is sure to come between, more so in a Year of the Tiger!

So they must decide whether they wish to be real friends and partners or whether they want to be adversaries. The Metal element of Rooster can transform the Wood of Tiger into something precious and valuable. Indeed, in 2010, Rooster is riding extremely high, having a very good year. Rooster benefits from the Star of Victory that brings triumphant moments. In its horoscope chart, the Rooster has almost perfect luck forces, especially 53 year old Fire Rooster and 17 year old Water Rooster.

Tiger's luck is not nearly as impressive. It is plagued by health afflictions so cannot be as strong or as productive as Rooster in 2010. This is certain to have a bearing on their respective roles within any Tiger/Rooster relationship. And being strong willed and highly individualistic, it is not easy to give way on the domestic front. So they must sort out their ego issues before they can live happily together this year.

TIGER WITH DOG *(Dependable)*
Trustworthy & Reliable

In a year when friendships are tested, these allies of the zodiac will thankfully stay true to one another. The Tiger and Dog need each other this year and one will find in the other a true and trustworthy friend. For a start, Tiger will discover Dog is as dependable and as loyal as ever, and Dog in turn will find that Tiger can be relied on when the going gets rough. Their allegiance to one another stays steadfast in what looks like a challenging year for both.

The Tiger and Dog are weakened by the ferocity of the year's conflicting energy patterns. Tiger is vulnerable to the illness star and suffers from a weakened life force. Dog has double negatives in its Life Force and Inner Essence. Dog people are beset with disappointments through the year, as zodiac enemies cause some havoc in their lives. In the end, it is allies like Tiger who will make them happy and give them support. So with Dog, Tiger has a chance to demonstrate its qualities of devotion and loyalty.

Those married to one another will find that by simply standing together in 2010 they can stand very tall indeed! This is because in 2010, the two signs' numbers in the feng shui chart enjoy what we refer to as the *Ho Tu* combination – these are the numbers 2 and

9 which indicate that as a team, the Tiger (2) and the Dog (9) can create something worthwhile. They will not only give strength to each other but can also develop something with significant long term gains.

The Ho Tu combination always brings good fortune. So although individually their luck does not look very good, together they manifest strong energy. They are definitely very favorable for each other this year, probably also because they have a knack for bringing out the best in each other. There is genuine love and understanding freely flowing between these two souls. There are no competitive issues or other pressures to cause tension. So happiness is something they will have.

The Tiger and Dog are extroverts who make friends easily. They make a great team in business, quite formidably transforming commercial buddies into life long personal friends. Over time, they build an impressive network of influential and meaningful contacts. Working together also brings them closer. They cherish similar principles and values, so strong bonding takes place at far deeper levels than is at first obvious.

TIGER WITH BOAR *(Stimulating)*
Secret Friends with Excellent Ho Tu

With the Boar, Tiger has a great and extremely satisfying relationship, and in 2010, they will find exhilarating companionship with one another. It will be a year when they discover just how stimulating they each can be as they inspire one another to overcome the negativities of the year and go forward bravely and surely. What is needed is confidence and reassurance and since they can rely on each other, the year can turn out to be exciting for them indeed.

These two are not just secret friends of the zodiac but in 2010, they also enjoy the added benefits of having their feng shui numbers create the auspicious Ho Tu combination. In the feng shui chart, Tiger is 2 and Boar is 9 and 2/9 combines to bring good news for the pair.

Th 2/9 Ho Tu brings them unexpected good fortune, and the Ho Tu is also powerful enough to override all other negative afflictions. What this means is that as a couple, the Tiger and Boar can quite effectively overcome whatever negativities may be brought to them as a result of feng shui afflictions and element mismatches.

Even without the Ho Tu they are already one of the more successful pairings of the zodiac. The Tiger and Boar enjoy very similar attitudes. They can see the good side of any development, and are good at making the best of whatever comes their way. They are positive people who know how to extract good energy from challenging times. The year is going to be a challenging one for many, but together, they can ride out any challenges they may encounter.

Indeed Boar's horoscope chart does not show very good indications. Neither is Tiger's chart looking particularly good; nevertheless, they will not suffer very negative swings in fortune in 2010.

The good thing about the Tiger and Boar union is how secure they are with each other. They do not have hidden agendas, nor do they harbor childish suspicions that lead to tensions and recriminations. Theirs is a very straightforward relationship where a lifetime commitment to one another is an easy thing.

Those of you in your twenties should get as much as you can out of the Tiger Year. There is money to be made and fortunes to be built. 2010 is as good a year as any to get started; and if you are lucky enough to be in a relationship with a Boar, make the most of it.

Part 3
Monthly Outlook

The coming year will not be an easy one for the Tiger. There are many challenges ahead, with predictions of poor health and unfortunate luck in relationships. Obstacles pop up to disrupt your plans, making tasks you undertake frustrating and wearisome. Tigers who work in big corporations may have to battle nasty politicking at the workplace, so will have to keep their wits about them. However, Tiger people are known for their resilience and tenacity, so don't let minor troubles stop you from achieving success. There is success to be had; you just need to get your timing right. Plan important activities only during months when you are strong. And enlist the help of a **Pi Yao** to appease the God of the Year who resides in your sector.

1ST MONTH
February 4th - March 5th 2010

FROM THE START A CHALLENGING YEAR

The year does not start all that well for the Tiger. The monthly five yellow makes an appearance bringing with it misfortune and illness. The Tiger needs the Water element and the Dragon to nullify the ill effects of the chi of the month. Try wearing the colors black and blue when you can. Also carry a Dragon amulet or wear the Dragon as jewellery. This is a month when you must not make new investments. It is very easy to lose money at a time like this. It is also better to stay low key. Avoid travel. Those in business should not expand.

WORK & CAREER – *Don't Engage In Gossip*

The office won't be your favorite place this month. It is easy to get sucked into the rumor mill, and worse still if you find yourself the main target. Don't engage in gossip or your words could get twisted and used against you. Avoid becoming overly cozy with co-workers you don't know too well. You don't know who you can trust and it is easy to be betrayed or played out when your chi is down. Take your work seriously or your boss may notice. Avoid turning up late and put in as much effort as the next guy if you have your sights set on that promotion later in the year.

BUSINESS — *Postpone Important Decisions*

Try to lie low and postpone important decisions. This is not time to make hasty switches in strategy even if things may not be going quite the way you'd like. Your wealth luck is limited this month, so you may want to boost this by placing a **wealth ship** sailing into your office and also into your home. If you already have a wealth ship, add a few more gold bars or ingots to signify some extra cargo for a month that appears to be slow in terms of business.

Use this as a time to consolidate and plan for the future. Play your cards close to your chest. Do not trust outsiders with trade secrets and upcoming plans. There could be a spy among you, so keep your eye out. Although there is no need to become paranoid, it is better to be forewarned thus forearmed. Focus on team building this month. You need to make sure that everyone who works for you is on your side.

LOVE & RELATIONSHIPS — *Be Mysterious*

When it comes to love, don't be an open book. A little mystery will get you a long way. If you want to bend your partner to your way of thinking, use persuasion rather than temper tantrums. Whispers not shouts will win the day. But if you just can't get yourself into the mood, save the romance for another time. If you cannot put your whole heart into something, it may be better not to attempt it. When it comes to principles, sometimes it is important to stick by them. You can agree to disagree, but do not allow yourself to be talked into going with something you instinctively know is wrong.

PERSONAL HEALTH — *Be Careful*
Health might become an issue this month, especially for elderly Tigers. Arm yourself with a **Wu Lou** or wear the **longevity symbol,** and don't take unnecessary risks when it comes to your health. Avoid staying in the NE sector which is very afflicted this month.

EDUCATION — *Schedule Your Time*
There may be some sacrifices to be made if you are serious about doing well in school. But if you work up the mentality to do well, your work will become as fun as your play. If you find your energy levels sagging, learn to schedule your time better. Falling sick could be a nuisance this month, especially if you happen to have a lot on your plate, so make an effort to keep up your resistance levels by sleeping early, eating well and leading a healthy lifestyle.

2ND MONTH
March 6th - April 4th 2010

GOOD LUCK FOR THOSE STUDYING

The month ahead looks promising for young Tigers in school. Creativity levels are high and it is easy to find the motivation to get all your work done early. This is also a good month when it comes to love and romance. Business luck also improves, as does career luck. However, watch out for tensions in the household. There may be disharmony arising from conflicts between family members. The best way to deal with this is to display six crystal balls in the center of the home. You should also try to be more understanding when it comes to other people's viewpoints.

WORK & CAREER — *Substance Matters*

What you know becomes especially important this month. Being a good talker won't be nearly enough right now, so use what spare time you have to get yourself well read and well informed. If you are serious about getting ahead in your career, it will be substance that counts. You can make this month work for you if you constantly have the answers when they are asked. The good news is you don't even have to be super intelligent to have them, just a little bit more hardworking than usual. Once you get yourself in the right mindframe, you will find it easy to motivate yourself.

BUSINESS — *Look at The Big Picture*
When making decisions, make sure all of your decisions are well-informed ones. Try not to go with instincts as that's not going to work right now. Make time to be as clued-up as possible in all the different aspects of your business. Your employees will be looking to you for guidance, so make sure that when you give it, it is good guidance. Ultimately, you will have to take responsibility for the decisions you make; this month it will be harder to pass the buck. Keep abreast of what's going on with the competition; as long as you have the big picture, there's little that will go too far wrong. What will get you is leaving everything to others. Keep your hands on the steering wheel this month if you want things to work out.

LOVE & RELATIONSHIPS — *Danger of Infidelity*
There is plenty of passion simmering, but this is generally better for Tigers who are single than married ones. If you are happily attached, there is some danger of infidelity, either on your part or the part of your spouse. It is important therefore to be understanding inside your relationship, and recognize predatory advances from outsiders for what they are. Don't let

yourself be the one to succumb to temptation or you will live to regret it. For those in relationships, it is worthwhile to wear the double happiness symbol this month, to safeguard your union from third party interference and other daily pressures.

FAMILY & HOME – *Stressful*

Relationships within the family unit could get noisy this month. There are tensions in the household arising from in-laws. If you are being pulled in different directions, use your own judgment when making decisions. You may find you need to be more diplomatic than usual to keep from going insane. But whatever you do, try not to fan the fire by being stubborn or difficult. When things get heated, it may be best to leave the house to air your head than risk saying something you may regret.

EDUCATION – *Listen to Others*

Anything to do with learning, research or expressing yourself will go well this month. Set yourself high standards because your chances of reaching them are high. When others offer you help, accept. You may think you can do it yourself, but giving others a little of your time just to hear what they have to say could open up whole new possibilities for you.

3RD MONTH
April 5th - May 5th 2010

LEGAL PROBLEMS & CONFLICTS

The quarrelsome star makes an appearance, causing you to have a shorter fuse than usual. You're going to have to make an extra effort to hold your temper because every little thing will seem to annoy you. While it may be strangely satisfying to be generally disagreeable, if you don't stop yourself, you may end up going too far. Once you cross the line it may be hard to go back, so don't let it get to that stage. The best advice this month is to lay low. Spend the month as quietly as possible and wait for the quarrelsome energy to blow over.

WORK & CAREER — *Working Well Alone*

This month you're better off working alone. With less interaction with colleagues, you reduce the possibility of misunderstandings. You'll find yourself extremely productive as a solo player, so attempt things on your own. No need to shut others out but don't engage in lengthy discussions with your workmates. It will only serve to get your hackles up. Keep a **Dragon Tortoise** behind you at work to ensure you retain the support of your boss, but the rule's the same when it comes to interaction with your superiors. The less the better as you're not at your best this month.

BUSINESS — *Red Tape*

Business may not go as smoothly as you'd like. There is a high probability of legal problems exploding into a serious matter. Don't get caught up with the law. Redtape could be a real nuisance when trying to do business this month, but live with it rather than complain, or you could find things becoming worse instead of better. If you're unlucky enough to have a legal case pending, the advice is to settle out of court. You cannot win with your energies like this, unless you can try to postpone any hearing to June, when you enjoy better luck.

LOVE & RELATIONSHIPS — *Learn to Laugh*

Don't expect a peaceful month when it comes to relationships. You could find yourself facing many disagreements, especially if you and your partner have been together for a long time. Don't turn something trivial into something serious. Learn to laugh at yourself and let go. In months like these, a sense of humor would probably be your best asset.

Those not already in a relationship should concentrate on other areas of their lives for the moment. Love and relationships are not up your street for the energies are not conducive. And making the wrong impression to someone you are interested in could spoil your chances for the future.

FAMILY & HOME — *Relax*

Rowing with the rest of the family ought to come as no surprise to you this month. You are irritable and short-tempered, and it is will be those closest to you that will get the brunt of your bad mood when you're in one. Concentrate on getting yourself to relax rather than getting involved in what everyone else is doing. Because you will tend to be stubborn and inflexible this month, your family members are unlikely to want your opinions and advice on whatever they are doing, so leave them alone. If you have to find yourself a new hobby to keep yourself occupied, go try something new. It could be just what the doctor ordered.

SCHOOL & EDUCATION — *Minor Aggravations*

Feelings of betrayal overtake you this month. Learn to ignore these aggravations. Things that seem very important now will seem truly insignificant a while later, so don't let anything get you down. If you feel betrayed by a close friend, find some distance between you for a while. Time will heal any wounds. Just don't try to rush things.

4TH MONTH
May 6th - June 5th 2010

DANGER OF ILLNESS & WIND DISEASES

This will not be an easy month for the Tiger. You become especially vulnerable to sickness and disease, so whatever you do, avoid travel to high risk places, avoid hospitals and other sites that are overly yin, and just be more careful in general. Pay more attention to hygiene, and take any medical warning bells seriously. If you find yourself falling sick, make sure you are not sleeping in the NE sector of the house, as this area is badly afflicted.

WORK & CAREER — *Short Tempers*

Workplace tensions may be getting you down this month. Short tempers causes more arguments than usual. You may also find yourself more tired than usual. Learn to let others help you if that's what you need. While you may be competitive by nature, this month, learn to work with others. You could find a different side of your personality which you end up preferring! Watch out for careless mistakes though.

Physically you are not at your strongest, and getting tired could cause you to let things slip by. If you make a mistake, take responsibility for it, but even better if you can avoid the mistake in the first place.

BUSINESS — *Conserve Cash*
You have little luck when it comes to wealth this month. Conserve your cash and consolidate your resources. It is better to stay liquid at a time when things are prone to going wrong. New projects started with the intention of expanding your channels of income may not work out the way you want.

Be prepared for surprises and don't be too stunned when things go wrong. However, keep your thumb on the pulse and watch you're not neglecting your business. Your staff will be looking to you for leadership, so lead them well. Display a statue of **Kuan Kung** in your office to improve business luck when turnover is slow.

FRIENDSHIPS & SOCIAL LIFE — *Toned Down*
You tend to enjoy your own company more than the company of others this month. This does not mean you don't like a good party, but time spent curled up in your living room with a good book will be just as satisfactory. Give yourself the alone time you need right now. You'll be back to your bubbly self next month, but some quiet time will provide a good balance of yin and yang in your life.

LOVE & ROMANCE — *Flirty Not Serious*

Luck in love is better than luck in money, especially for the single male Tiger. Tiger guys have it better than the girls this month. Tiger females are in danger of catching some unsavory disease, so it is better to err on the side of caution. Lasting relationships are unlikely to be struck up this month, although there's plenty of fun to be had by those not looking for anything serious.

EDUCATION — *Avoid Breaking Rules*

This is not a great month for the young Tiger. Watch the company you keep. It is easy to fall under the influence of unsuitable friends. Listen to your parents if they notice something amiss whether it's the company you're keeping, your behaviour or your attitude. They have your best interest at heart. Don't let yourself be pressurized into doing something out of peer pressure. If you feel it is wrong, stick by your principles and be strong. Avoid playing pranks and doing anything against the rules; the consequences could be direr than you expect.

The illness energies are strong this month. Display longevity symbols in the NE of the house or wear against the body.

5TH MONTH
June 6th - July 6th 2010

VICTORY LUCK WITH GOOD NEWS AT WORK

Your luck improves significantly this month. If you've been worrying about money, something will happen to alleviate those worries. Business luck improves and there is good news at work. While in general you luck is good, expect to face fierce competition. However, you have victory luck on your side, so if you maintain your cunning and work at strategy, success is relatively easy to come by this month. Be prepared to take some risks if you want to leapfrog to the next stage, whether in your career or in business. Be brave because this is when courage will stand you in good stead.

WORK & CAREER – *Change is Possible*

Those employed in jobs they genuinely enjoy will do well this month. But if you're in a profession where your only motivation is earning that salary to put food on the table, you may find yourself looking at alternatives. This is a month when change is eminently possible, and even beneficial, so if you feel you are stuck in a rut, stop feeling sorry for yourself and start thinking about what you can do about it.

BUSINESS – *Change Meetings*

You have good "influence luck" this month, meaning that others will listen to what you say and take you seriously. They may even act on your suggestions. Use this skill well. Make use of your network of friends and associates to help you where you need. You may also have chance meetings with certain individuals who may suddenly make your plans more seemingly achievable. Follow up on new leads. You'll be surprised how easy it is to achieve something if you keep persevering.

Look out for new opportunities to pursue. A host of them will present themselves if you keep your eyes and ears open. This is a good time to go into something new. The energy of the month favors starting new things, changing direction and business expansion, so start thinking along those lines.

LOVE & RELATIONSHIPS – *Long Term Prospects*

For the single Tiger, this month will see you more interested in the long term prospects of your relationships than short term ones. If you're thinking of settling down with someone, act on it. Your overtures will be well received and there is happiness to be had here. Married Tigers however need to be more careful, as you could suffer from some heartache on this front. Watch out for troublesome third parties who could make their way into your life and upset an otherwise idyllic home situation. If you are alert to the dangers from the start, you can nip them in the bud. Place an **amethyst crystal** under the bed on the left hand side tied with red string, particularly if you are the female in the relationship.

SCHOOL & EDUCATION — *Recognition*

Schoolwork goes well this month. Your results and efforts will be recognized, and if you're good enough, you may soon be presented with some kind of award to formally commend your efforts. In the meantime, continue to put wholehearted effort into your schoolwork. Once you get into the swing of studying, it is easy to continue on that same productive mode.

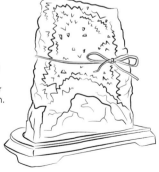

Place an amethyst crystal tied with red string under the bed to protect your marriage this month.

6TH MONTH
July 7th - Aug 7th 2010

ENERGY LEVELS ARE LOW

The magnifying 9 flies into your chart this month, exarcerbating the illness affliction that plagues you this year. This causes your energy levels to weaken, making you once again vulnerable to falling sick or feeling listless and tired. Keep up the momentum if you find your energy levels flagging. If you succumb to flagging energy, you could get caught in a downward spiral. What you need this month is a strong wu lou amulet. Get one of suitable size made of brass and display by your bedside or in the NE part of your home or bedroom. And make health and wellness a priority this month.

WORK & CAREER — *Creativity Dries Up*

Creativity dries up at work this month, making it harder to output. You're kept busy, if not from actual productive work, then from dodging potshots from jealous workmates. There are vultures in your midst waiting to pounce on your scraps should you make a mistake. Your biggest danger is carelessness from lack of concentration. This all stems from your weakened energy levels. Engage in activities outside of work that rejuvenate you. Keep healthy by maintaining a balance in your life. Exercise is important. If you work long hours and never see daylight except through the window, your health is going to suffer. You may have to reorientate your workday to accomodate this plan. Put in some effort organizing yourself better, and there will be significant improvement in your work productivity.

BUSINESS — *Strong Competition*

You may face strong competition in business this month and as a result see revenues start to dip. Carelessness may allow industry rivals to get ahead. Spend more time working on marketing activities, and if you're in a service-oriented industry, you may want to re-look at customer relations. If you've been neglecting the business because things have been going well, you may have to rethink this strategy.

LOVE & ROMANCE — *Vulnerable Time*

Beware of illicit affairs this month. If you've been going through a difficult time, you may be more vulnerable to the charms of someone who takes advantage of this. Because your chi energy is low, your judgment may also be off; if so, take advice from family and close friends who have your best interests at heart. When it comes to new romances, it is better to take things slow. Rushing headlong into a helter skelter relationship could lead to something you regret quite soon after. For married Tigers, don't take your spouse for granted. You may be in a grouchy frame of mind, and they may put up with you, but try not to push them too far.

HEALTH — *Poorly*

Your health is poorly this month and something you should put more attention on. You could fall ill or catch a disease, and if left untreated, this could escalate into something more serious quite quickly. Don't take any risks when it comes to your health this month. Avoid the NE sector which has a congregation of dangerous stars this month, especially if you are elderly, weak or unhealthy. It is better to move out of the NE if your bedroom is here than to take chances.

SCHOOL & EDUCATION — *Focus Your Attention*

Schoolwork won't be the only thing on your mind this month. You may have family issues to deal with or a big occasion coming up in one of your extracurricular activities. Watch you don't have too much on your plate. Fight the tendency to be scatterbrained. Slow down on the extracurriculars if you find it is affecting your schoolwork.

7TH MONTH
Aug 8th - Sept 7th 2010

EXCELLENT MONTH
WHEN EVERYTHING BENEFITS

Things don't get much better than this! Whether you're a professional or entrepreneur, there's plenty of room for your creative input. Ideas spark up in your head, and translating them into reality will happen as a matter of course. There is wealth luck indicated and at the workplace, there is strong indication of upward mobility.

You enjoy the excellent sum-of-ten combination where everything benefits, so you can go ahead with your plans confidently this month. Take full advantage of the lucky stars in your chart this month by keeping busy.

WORK & CAREER — *Seize Initiative*

Work is pleasant this month. You feel more alive and capable of handling whatever you are put in charge of. but when your luck is this good, you don't want to just get by. You want to stand out. Make your superiors sit up and take notice of you. To do that you need to do not just a good job but an outstanding job. Seize the initiative and impress the pants off the right people. You have promotion luck but only if you work for it.

Make sure you don't waste the opportunity! Boost career luck by placing a Dragon Tortoise behind your desk at work. The Dragon Tortoise will give you the support you need to push your ideas through, making people listen to you. It will also help ensure your ideas are sound.

BUSINESS — *Prosperity Luck*

Prosperity luck benefits Tigers in business this month. Opportunities of wealth creation are abundant. You feel more ambitious than usual and for good reason. There is market share to tap out there. If you are in sales, make your sales pitches this month. Squeeze in as many appointments as you can. Boost your marketing efforts because you want to market when luck is on your side. In times when your luck is good, spare a thought for donating to charity. Donating a portion of your earnings will ensure your good fortune is long-lived.

LOVE & RELATIONSHIPS — *Follow Your Heart*

Love is in the air! Your feelings for someone in particular may overwhelm you. This is a month when it pays to follow your heart. Listen to your intuition when it comes to saying yes or no to somebody. You have good instincts this month, so follow them. Learn to be more vocal about your feelings; if you care for somebody, tell them so.

While action speaks louder than words, it is still nice to be told once in a while.

HOME & FAMILY — *Cozy*

The family unit is strong this month. This is a good time to get in touch with distant relatives you haven't seen or spoken to in a while. You will have plenty to catch up on, and you may find new things in common that you didn't have before. If you've been wanting to build up rapport with the in-laws, this is a fruitful time to do it. Be the one to initiate things.

EDUCATION — *Guidance from Mentor*

This will be an easy month for Tigers in school. It is easy to stay on top of things, and you benefit from encouragement from teachers. If you have a mentor figure, it may be useful to tap their brain at this time. You are mentally resilient this month, so any helpful advice will only make you stronger. You are in a good position to benefit from good guidance as you can see the wood for the trees. Make the best use of this time by drawing on all your available resources.

Place a Dragon Tortoise on your desk to maintain the support of your boss and the people you work with.

8TH MONTH
Sept 8th - Oct 7th 2010

IGNORE GOSSIP & OFFICE POLITICKING

This is a dangerous month as the violent star flies into your chart. Be careful of people out to harm you. There is betrayal luck in your chart, which means you could be cheated over money, or even let down by friends and people you trust. Rely on yourself rather than others this month.

Stay aloof to issues and other people's problems. Don't offer your advice unless you are asked for it. Above all things, don't engage in tittle-tattle or you'll find yourself the one being hurt in the end. At work, expect to put up with some gossip, but learn to ignore it. If you react, things will turn out worse. Wear the **Elephant Amulet** to protect against the negative energies of the month.

WORK & CAREER — *Office Politics*

Office politics may once again rear its ugly head. Stay neutral and do not let yourself be talked into joining a particular camp. You could regret it deeply when you discover you backed the wrong horse. Keep your opinions to yourself and do not reveal too much. You don't know who is on your side. Your best bet this month is to focus on your work. Keep that as your priority and you shouldn't go too far wrong.

Avoid gossip at the workplace. Do not be duped into giving your opinion when you don't have to. Indulging in small talk may cause you to slip up and reveal too much. Things are not what they seem. Although the intention may not be to catch you out, if you don't watch your step you may unintentionally give someone something to use against you when it benefits them. Don't trust people this month. Learn to trust yourself.

BUSINESS — *Avoid Arguments*
Think about long-term goals over short-term ones. Disagreements with your business associates and partners should be handled with care. Do not rile those you work with for no reason. Avoid arguing over matters that are personal in nature. Getting personal is unprofessional and won't get you anywhere.

Keep yourself open to new ideas. Remember that your opinions will evolve and change. Disagreeing vehemently over something only to change your mind later will make you look fickle and erratic. When you are unsure about something, keep your opinions to yourself. Saying too little is better than saying too much right now.

LOVE & RELATIONSHIPS — *Stressful Time*

Things will not be easy in love. The metal chi this month is very strong and you need to counter that by controlling your emotions. Fighting with your loved ones won't get you anywhere. Be ready to apologize or accept an apology. Avoid double dating this month, or your dating buddy could snatch your date from under your nose! If there is someone special you are pursuing, it is best not to initiate him or her into your group of friends just yet, especially if things are still new with the both of you.

PERSONAL SAFETY — *Beware of Snatch Thieves*

Take safety seriously this month. Carry a **Blue Rhinoceros and Elephant Amulet** to ward off risk of robbery and snatch thieves. Remember to lock up at night, and don't take any chances when it comes to security issues. Try not to put yourself in a dangerous situation. Avoid dark alleyways, deserted carparks and other such danger hotzones, particularly if you are female.

Be more careful when it comes to personal safety this month. Carry the Blue Rhinoceros and Elephant Amulet to protect against muggers.

9TH MONTH
Oct 8th - Nov 6th 2010

POWER RETURNS TO YOU AT WORK

Luck improves for you this month and office life becomes more pleasant. You gain new respect from your peers and become a valuable member of the team. Camaradie with others improves and there is the possibility of someone influential helping you. You have excellent mentor luck on your side. Heaven smiles on you, so if there are dreams and goals you want to pursue, you can make a real go at them this month. Trust your instincts and let your inspiration take over. You have divine help bringing you unexpected good fortune.

WORK & CAREER — *Showcase Your Abilities*

If you have good ideas, share them. Your contribution at work will prove valuable this month, so don't let your talents go to waste by being overly humble. This is a time to showcase your abilities and hope the right person spots it. You have just the right kind of luck on your side this month, so it would be a shame not to make the most of it. Working with others comes naturally to you this month, and you also make an excelletn leader. There is promotion luck on the cards, but you must follow through if you are serious about advancing up the career ladder. If you choose to put your heart in your work and career this month, you can make good headway.

BUSINESS — *New Opportunities*

You enjoy excellent new business prospects this month. But while opportunities may present themselves, they will only reap their benefits if you follow through with them. Success will come to the Tiger who is proactive about following up on leads. Make use of your contacts built up over the years. You may have to call on the help of an old friend. Pick up the phone and you'll be surprised to find how quickly things start to work themselves out. Don't be reclusive when your relationship luck with others is so good. This is a time to make new friends or rekindle old friendships. If someone tries to interest you in a new project, take the suggestion seriously and investigate. This month a new opportunity that comes holds out the promise of power and financial gain. Don't let it pass you by.

LOVE & RELATIONSHIPS — *A Happy Time!*

There is success in love for the Tiger this month. You feel much more contentment with life and this makes you an easy companion. Others will naturally gravitate towards you, so this is a good time to make new friends. Love relationships in particular go very well.

There is a chance of falling for someone older than you, but as long as you are not being taken advantage of, there could be something special here. If you're married, make the most of this time to spend some quality time with your better half. Book yourself on that holiday you've always wanted to take together; this will be a great way to rekindle the passion in your relationship!

EDUCATION — *Seek Counsel*

For the young Tiger in school, there are many opportunities for growth this month. You will grow intellectually as well as as a person. Take on a mentor figure if you have someone suitable in mind. If you're lucky enough to find the right mentor, this month is a treasure trove of opportunities. For those of you facing some important decisions, don't forget to seek counsel. Someone older and more experienced guiding you will make all the difference to you coming to the right decision.

10TH MONTH
Nov 7th - Dec 6th 2010

FIVE YELLOW CAUSES SOME DIFFICULTIES
This could be a dangerous month for the
Tiger with the Five Yellow flying in to cause
some havoc. The misfortune star attracts
problems and accidents. You could find
obstacles popping up to obstruct an otherwise
straightforward task or deal you are doing.
Simple things go wrong, and there is the
possibility to lose money even for the risk-averse
Tiger. Avoid investing heavily and definitely stay
away from gambling in any form. It is best to
avoid new ventures. Stay low key and avoid
socializing excessively this month.

WORK & CAREER — *Depleted Energy*
Be prepared to face some challenges at work. The
month won't be an easy one and you could find
yourself pushed to the limits. Avoid confrontations
with co-workers, as this will further drain your already
depleted energy. Illness brings distractions and delays
to your projects. If you are working to tight deadlines,
plan ahead to avoid last minute panic attacks. Anxiety
could take a toll on your health, so try not to get
yourself overly worked up over things. There may

be some stress caused by office tittle-tattle. The best response is to resist the temptation to gossip yourself, or you could end up becoming the main target. Wear the **5 Element Pagoda** as a charm of pendant, or carry one with you, to counter the negative energies of the month. You are in danger of saying the wrong things, so think before you speak. In meetings and group discussion, don't volunteer too much information if you are unsure of your facts.

BUSINESS – *Lay Low*
This is not a good time to go into new ventures or to invest heavily. Use this period to consolidate and plan for the future, but resist executing any plans that involve heavy financial outlay for now. Your luck is down and it is easy to lose money. You may have to think outside the box to survive and difficult period but the more you work those brain cells, the more efficient they become. Unexpected obstacles may arise, putting a spanner in the works for some pet project of yours. Don't get emotionally attached to anything. If it is time to cut your losses, it may be better to do it.

LOVE & RELATIONSHIPS – *Not Great*
You may have many fanciful ideas when it comes to love and romance, but this is a time when you could be in for a disappointment. For Tigers who are single, this may not be the best time to be courting. If you plan

to make the big moves, better to wait till next month. Avoid formalizing any relationship this month for your luck does not bode well if you're hoping for something that will last into the future. Definitely avoid this month when it comes to weddings.

EDUCATION — *You Benefit from Alone Time*
You may feel inadequate socially, find yourself saying the wrong things or upsetting others unintentionally. It may be a good time for some time alone to improve your mood and demeanor. If you don't feel like hanging out with your friends, don't! You don't always need to do what is expected of you. Worse if you unleash your foul mood on the people around you.

PERSONAL SAFETY — *Stay in Your Comfort Zone*
If you're active in contact or high risk sports, be a bit more careful this month. This is not a good time to be overly brave. Stay in your comfort zone in whatever you partake in, and don't let other people egg you on into doing something you're uncomfortable with. Wear the color white to counter the fierce Metal energy of the month.

11TH MONTH
Dec 7th - Jan 5th 2011

YOUNG COUPLES ENJOY A ROMANTIC TIME

Romance takes center stage this month when the Tiger looking for love will find no shortage of suitors. There are amorous feelings all around. However beware you don't do anything reckless in a moment of weakness. Keep your wits about you, especially when there are drinks around.Study luck is also good, so young Tigers in school will find some respite from a difficult last month. Watch however for tensions and strained relations at home. You may have to be a bit more understanding when it comes to your relationships with family, especially in-laws. A little understanding goes a long way.

WORK & CAREER — *Things Proceed Smoothly*

The way you deal with others becomes especially important this month, and will have a large bearing on your chances to move ahead in your career. Relationship luck is strong and effort made on your part will be more than reciprocated. Your views may differ from those of your colleagues and co-workers, but as long as you can come to a happy compromise, things proceed smoothly for you. This month particularly favors Tigers working in the communications and media industries. Those whose jobs involve writing or research will do especially well. Try not to be overly intimidating when putting your ideas across if you want your opinions to be taken well. The forceful method does not work so well this month. Instead, try using charm and persuasion and you will get far.

BUSINESS — *Stay Calm*

Don't let problems stress you out. Whatever dilemmas you may be facing can be overcome if you deal with them with a clear head. Avoid the panic syndrome when dealing with deadlines. The more you worry, the worse your abilities with dealing with whatever you have on your plate.

If you have overextended yourself, make an effort to stay calm and put a systematic plan into action. Allies are important to the Tiger person this month, so don't make enemies unnecessarily. Note that your people skills are particularly favorable this month. Schedule face-to-face meetings rather than phonecalls or emails. These are more personal and this way you can work your charm, which will get you a long way.

LOVE & RELATIONSHIPS — *Lucky in Love*

This is a promising month for romance. Tigers in relationships enjoy good fortune, and you will tend to be luckier if you have a special someone supporting you. Give your partner credit where it's due. It is always nice to be appreciated.

Single Tigers will have no problem finding suitors. Whether or not anything more serious developes depends on how far you want to take things. You can crystallize romance luck by wearing the **double happiness symbol**. Watch however for third party troublemakers. If you are happily married or engaged, don't let outsiders sully your relationship with your partner by putting ideas in your head. When it comes to trusting people, it is better to trust your own family.

EDUCATION — *Sociable*
A lucky month awaits the young Tiger in school and those studying or involved in research. Remember to maintain a balance in your life. If you want your academic work to go well, get enough rest and incorporate other activities in your life. Because social luck is good this month, try not to fall into the hermit trap. Burrowing yourself in research won't get you nearly as far as if you mixed and mingled with company. Be sociable. Friends in your life right now will be good for your work and good for your soul.

12TH MONTH
Jan 6th - Feb 3rd 2011

WEAR RED & STAY ALOOF

The argument star makes an appearance causing this to be a quarrelsome month for the Tiger. Your temper is short and the smallest thing can set you off. Legal problems surface and at work you may have to deal with office politics. What you need this month is the **Fire Sword** to cut away at malicious and harmful gossip. Don't get too close to people you don't know too well this month. Keep "friends" at arm's length. If someone tries to get too close, question their motives. They may be real, but it is better to be careful in a month when this aspect of your luck is down.

WORK & CAREER — *Think Before You Speak*

This month is an irritable one for you when you won't suffer fools gladly. Others miss your good intentions, especially if you're too sharp with your words. Watch how you come across as you wouldn't want to project the wrong impression. Because you are prickly this month, it may be better to avoid important meetings. Saying the wrong things could become an annoying mistake. Think before you speak, and don't engage in too much meaningless conversation. Lay low and don't appear threatening to your co-workers; they may see you as competition and then all claws will be out. You may need to make a good impression this month; to do this, learn to be a good listener. Putting your ideas across may be important, but right now what is more important is to appear to be a good team player that can fit in with others. You are worth more in how you fit into the whole scheme of things - so even if you have grand plans to become the "leader", keep them to yourself right now. Your time will come when your luck improves. For now, wear red and stay aloof.

BUSINESS — *Stay Modest*

Business suffers from gossip this month. This is not helped by your unreasonable mood. Focus on the important tasks at hand, but leave dealmaking till another time. If there are important presentations to be made, it may be better if you stay out of them, leaving the job to your best general. Your tongue is a touch too acidic to win over whoever you are trying to impress. While you may have lofty ambitions, hold on to them till next month. Your luck is not great when it comes to going after anything big. Stay modest and put a hold on investments. Think how you can conserve rather than splash out. Don't get greedy or you will have cause for regret.

LOVE & RELATIONSHIPS — *Small Frustrations*

You may find yourself getting rubbed the wrong way more often than not. Arguments abound and you find it difficult to keep the peace. Avoid arguing over small things that don't matter. The more you argue, the more frustrated you will get, and the greater the chance of you saying something you will regret. If you are single, perhaps wait till a better time to find your perfect match. Your standards are too high right now, causing you to miss many good opportunities when it comes to matters of the heart. For now, focus on keeping your friends rather than desperately try to make new ones.

SCHOOL & EDUCATION — *Distractions*

Things are better for the Tiger in school. If you can stay single-minded about your studies, you can achieve a lot. What causes you angst this month are friendships. You may feel let down by a friend. Don't let something like that stress you out. Your relationships with others improve next month. For not, give others the benefit of the doubt. Stay out of gossiping or it could boomerang in your direction.

Part 4
Updating House Feng Shui

To maintain good feng shui in your home and to ensure a smooth transition into the new year, you need to add a **time dimension** to your use of feng shui. This means making some vital changes to the placement of decorative objects, making alterations to the way furniture is arranged in the public areas of your home and sometimes even making adjustments to room usage.

Making changes to accommodate the new annual chi is important to maintain a balance of good energy in the home. This is what will help residents enjoy a better year, as you are then protected against getting hit by nasty surprises and misfortune happenings.

The changes in energy each new year is something not many people are aware of, as a result of which, even when a home has been very well designed according to feng shui principles, when no effort is made to accommodate yearly changes of energy, sometimes bad luck descends unexpectedly, causing sudden problems to descend on the family; and often, misfortune brought by afflictive flying stars can be quite severe, serious enough to cause a high degree of stress and tribulations.

When unlucky energy inadvertently flies into the part of your home where your **main door** is located, or where your **bedroom** is sited, you and often your family as well risk being hit by some kind of misfortune. This may be a sudden illness, an unexpected accident or loss, a court case or a significant reversal of fortune that brings hardship. It is advisable to anticipate this kind of problem, address it and install remedies and cures. This is the best way to practice feng shui with great effectiveness.

The location and severity of **feng shui afflictions** that bring bad luck to residents are revealed by annual flying stars. These are numbers that move around a specially constructed **feng shui chart** based on an ancient formula that maps out the changing chi movements of each new year.

These changes alter the way the luck of any home plays out in any given year. It is part of the time aspect of feng shui and is something that should be incorporated into an annual renewal of chi program for the home. Attending to this ensures that the energy of abodes stay fresh and vigorous.

Yearly Feng Shui Afflictions

These bring negative luck, causing misfortune, accidents, loss and a variety of ills to manifest. This part of the book explains the severity and location of the different afflictions in the Year of the Tiger and highlights those of particular importance to those born in the Year of the Tiger. Once you know what and where the afflictions are, it is not difficult to deal with them using element cures and other powerful traditional feng shui methods.

It is important to subdue annual feng shui afflictions because these have the potential to create havoc in your life. Misfortune can come in a variety of ways. Sometimes they manifest as severe illness suffered by some member of the family; or they can cause loss of wealth, loss of good name or loss of a loved one. It is not difficult to control feng shui afflictions and doing so helps prevent bad luck from occurring, so everyone should really take the trouble to do so.

In the past, this aspect of feng shui practice was simply ignored by modern day practitioners, leaving many vulnerable to reversals of fortune, although in recent years, awareness of time dimension feng shui has increased substantially. Master practitioners of feng shui in Asia and around the world now go to great lengths to study, analyze and deal with time related feng shui afflictions at the start of each New Year.

The cut-off date when energy patterns change occurs around February 4th, which is regarded as the first day of Spring – in Chinese known as the *lap chun*. This is not to be confused with the lunar New Year date which is determined by the Chinese lunar calendar. The Chinese use their solar calendar (known as the *Hsia Calendar*) to track feng shui energy changes. The monthly change of energy patterns in Part 3 of the book, for instance, uses the Hsia calendar to determine the dates when each month starts.

The feng shui chart of any year is usually depicted in a 9 x 9 sector Lo Shu square with a number in each grid. These numbers are determined by the ruling or center number which in 2010 is 8. Once the center number is known, the rest of the numbers in the different grids of the Lo Shu square can be determined.

2010 Annual Feng Shui chart

SE	S	SW
7	3	5
6	8	1
2	4	9
NE	N	NW

E (left side)   W (right side)

The numbers in this chart change or "fly" from year to year, reflecting changes in energy in the different direction sectors. Each of the numbers in the different compass locations reveals the quality of energy ruling that location in 2010.

The numbers 1 through 9 in each of the nine grids of the Lo Shu Square offer insights into the way the pattern of luck has moved in any built up structure or building. This investigation precedes the updating of feng shui.

In addition to afflictions, the chart also reveals the good luck sectors - i.e. those parts of your house that enjoy the most auspicious luck during the year. If the lucky numbers fly into the sector that houses your main door or bedroom, or into any part of the home where you spend a considerable amount of time, then the good energy of that location will shower you with good fortune.

Sometimes the feng shui of your bedroom can be so good overrides any kind of low energy you may be suffering from your horoscope for the year. When auspicious numbers enter the location of your animal sign, it will benefit you for that year. Hence understanding the annual chart enables you to subdue bad luck and bad feng shui; and to enhance good luck and good feng shui.

> **When feng shui afflictions of your living and work spaces are treated with feng shui cures, and the lucky sectors are activated with auspicious decorative objects or celestial creatures, your luck for the year is sure to instantly improve.**

You can overcome obstacles to success more effectively, and make better decisions by tracking your luck through each month of the year. Timing plays a crucial role and when armed with prior knowledge of good and bad months, you are certain to have a positive competitive edge.

Updating your feng shui brings powerful benefits as you will know exactly how to be protected against sudden changes of fortunes. Those unprotected are vulnerable not only to annual afflictions but also to monthly ill winds that might be blowing your way.

It is so important then to know about good and bad months.

Misfortune usually comes suddenly, descending on you when least expected. It can come as illness, or manifest as court action, or worse, as some kind of personal loss. Misfortune can hit at anytime. Don't think that bad things do not happen to good people, because they do. Since it requires so little effort to guard against bad luck and bad feng shui, it seems foolish not to do so.

Luck of Different Parts of Home

The annual feng shui chart reveals the luck of every part of the house categorized into compass sectors based on their respective locations. So every compass corner of the home must be investigated. Each sector has a number from 1 through 9, and this comprises eight outer sectors plus the center. In 2010, the center sector ruling number is 8, and this allows the numbers of the outer 8 sectors to be identified.

These numbers enable a knowledgeable feng shui practitioner to instantly be able to identify afflicted sectors. These are the parts of the house where cures and remedies need to be put into place because doing so brings protection to the whole house!

In the same way, the luckiest sectors can also be ascertained and then activated to manifest good luck. When individual sectors get enhanced, the improved chi energy spreads to the rest of the house. It is therefore necessary to study the feng shui chart for 2010, and then superimpose it onto the layout sketches of your home, using a good compass to anchor the directions. Always remember to use a good compass to determine the compass sectors of your home.

> Familiarize yourself with the chart of 2010 and systematically list down the afflictions that are particularly harmful for your house. Remember that when bad luck numbers occur in rooms that you or your family use often, that is when placing the correct remedies and cures take on some urgency.

If the bad luck numbers fall into storerooms, toilets, kitchens or to parts of house that make up **missing corners**, then the misfortune bringing numbers should have little negative effect. When these bad luck numbers come into your bedroom, or afflict important doors and areas of the home (such as the dining area and family area) then once again, remedies become very important.

The same analogy applies to good luck stars. When these fly into important and heavy traffic rooms, the auspicious luck gets activated, and they then bring benefits to residents. When they enter into small rooms like store rooms or tight little alcoves in the home, their good effect does not benefit the household as much.

Activating Good Star Numbers

You need to remember that in Flying Star feng shui, good and bad luck numbers need to be activated either by placing an object that symbolizes a producing element (such as Water element producing Wood element in a Wood sector like East or SE) or with an auspicious decorative item.

Here, knowing what **celestial creature** to display and what **element** is favorable for the year will help you to vastly improve your feng shui. Other ways to activate good numbers is to increase the level of yang energy in the corners benefiting from the year's good fortune numbers. Thus using bright lights and increasing sound levels in the center of the house in 2010 should benefit the household greatly.

This is because the center plays host to the auspicious 8 and activating it is sure to bring benefits. In 2010, the center of the house should be energized by the presence of **multiple crystal balls** – eight is an excellent number. This strengthens the Earth element of the center and since 8 is itself an Earth element number, and considering that the earth element symbolizes wealth in 2010, enhancing Earth energy is excellent indeed.

Crystal balls of any kind will be very beneficial for the center of the home in 2010. The large **Tara Crystal Ball** which we brought out last year to energize 8 in the SE sector then was a great success for many people and for those who want to use these again this year, just move it to the center of the room. Make sure you twirl it daily because this activates the positive effects of crystal ball; as the ball contains the praises to the Goddess Tara, twirling the ball activates its wish-fulfilling aspect.

There is also another crystal ball which contains the powerful six syllable *Om Mani Padme Hum* mantra in Tibetan. For those wanting to create an aura of blessings in the home you can also place this **Om Mani Crystal Ball** in the center, or on the coffee table in the living room. A golden

8 embedded inside the crystal ball activates the power of 8. To make feng shui even more effective, keep light turned on as much as possible in the center of the home as Fire enhances Earth. Light combined with the action of twirling the ball ensures good positive yang energy gets generated. This draws auspicious energy into the home.

We have designed a beautiful **Crystal 8** with real gold flakes embedded within to be placed in the center of the home. This will add significantly to the enhancement of the Earth element which will be so beneficial in 2010. Another powerful enhancer which can be placed in the center of the home to activate the auspicious 8 is the **Victory Banner Windchime**.

Place the Victory Banner Windchime in the center of the house to activate the lucky 8.

Feng Shui Chart of 2010

The feng shui chart of 2010 is created by placing the ruling number of the year in the center. We have already taken note that the ruling number of the year is 8, and considering we are currently in the Period of 8, this makes the number 8 extremely significant and very lucky indeed.

2010 Year of the Golden Tiger

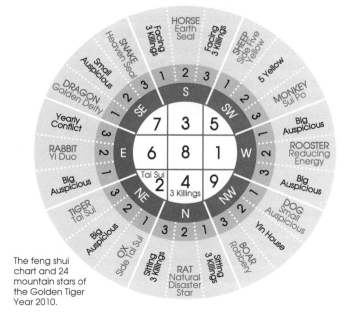

The feng shui chart and 24 mountain stars of the Golden Tiger Year 2010.

Activating the 8 in the center brings amazing good fortune and this is the reason why we are strongly recommending the crystal 8 with gold for the center of the house! Those whose Kua number or Lo Shu number is 8 can expect the year to go well for them, as this is also the period of 8.

This also includes women whose Kua number is 5. This is because Kua number 5 transforms to 8 for women. Just make sure you make an effort to activate the 8 in the center of the house.

You can check the Lo Shu and Kua numbers of your loved ones and friends from the resource tables contained in our *Feng Shui Diary 2010*. The chart of the year can be used to study the feng shui of any building, but you must use a compass to anchor the directions of the different rooms of your house or office. Then systematically investigate the luck of every sector.

Luck Stars of the 24 Mountains

In addition to numbers of the chart, we study the influences of the stars that fly into the 24 mountain directions of the compass. These "stars" do not carry the same weighting in terms of their strength and luck -bringing potential, but they add important nuances to annual chart readings, and are extracted from the Almanac. Incorporating the influence of the stars adds depth to a reading of the year's feng shui energy, and each of the twelve signs.

Together, the stars and the numbers reveal accurate things about the year, and when we add the influence of the year's elements, readings for each animal sign become very potent and exciting. This assists you to get the best from the year. The seamless merging of Chinese Zodiac Astrology with feng shui comprises the core strength and great value of our little astrology books, which we take great joy and pride in researching and writing every year.

This is the seventh year of our *Fortune & Feng Shui* list. Each year we delve a little deeper into all that influences the fortune and luck of the 12 animal signs, and the recommendations contained herein take account of these influences. Please use the analysis in this section to move from sector to sector and from room to room in your home, systematically installing feng shui remedies affected by bad chi energy. Place powerful decorative energizers and protective images to create and safeguard good luck.

ILLNESS STAR 2
Hits the Northeast in 2010

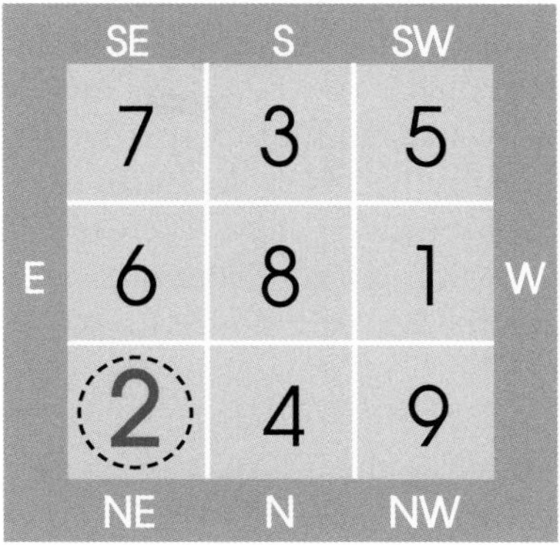

SE	S	SW
7	3	5
6	8	1
2	4	9
NE	N	NW

(E on left side, W on right side)

This is the Illness Star which flies to NE in 2010. The "star" brings propensity to getting sick for those whose bedroom or door is located in the NE sector of the home.

The illness star 2 flies to the NE in 2010. This is an Earth element sector and since the illness star 2 is an Earth element number, it makes the illness affliction extremely strong in the Year of the Tiger.

Earth flying into Earth suggests that those residing in the NE of their homes, or having an office or a front door in the NE, tend to be vulnerable to getting sick.

Unless the illness-bringing energy in this part of buildings is strongly suppressed, people residing or working in that part of the building are likely to develop physical ailments. And since the illness star is strong this year, it is harder to control.

The two animal signs affected by the illness star are the Tiger and Ox, who are Wood and Earth respectively. The Tiger's Wood is an effective foil to the Earth star of illness, but for the Ox, the illness star is likely to pose a serious health threat. It is a good idea not to spend too much time in the NE part of your living room or home.

If your bedroom is located in the NE of your house, make sure suitable remedies are placed here to suppress illness vibes. When the main door of the house is located in the NE, the constant opening and closing of the door is sure to activate the illness-bringing star. It is advisable to try and use another door located in another sector. If this is not possible, then try exhausting the Earth energy here. Remove all Earth element items such as crystals, porcelain vases or stone objects. Also keep lights here dim to reduce Fire element energy. This is because Fire strengthens Earth.

Cures for the Illness Star of 2010

There are excellent remedies that can be used to suppress the illness star. In 2010, a **Tiger/Dragon Wu Lou** would be especially effective. Another excellent cure is the **Antakarana Symbol** which is powerful enough to suppress the strong illness star this year, especially when it is made of metal. Brass is especially good as Metal exhausts the Earth energy of the illness star.

The symbol itself is a powerful symbol of healing and has a three dimensional effect that cuts directly into harmful negative energy. Get this symbol and place under the bed if your bed is located in the NE of your bedroom, or if your bedroom itself is in the NE.

Those born in the year of the Tiger are strongly advised to sleep with the symbol of the Antakarana under their pillows, or better yet, to wear the Antakarana ring preferably made in yellow gold. The energies emitted by the powerful Antakarana symbol – basically a trinity of 7 placed inside a circle - will effectively keep sickness at bay.

The healing symbol of Antahkarana.

LITIGATION STAR 3
Hits the South in 2010

	SE	S	SW	
	7	3	5	
E	6	8	1	W
	2	4	9	
	NE	N	NW	

This is the unlucky 3 Star which brings court case & quarrels. It flies to the South in 2010, affecting all of you whose room or office are located in the South. Use red or fire energy to suppress.

The quarrelsome star 3, which brings the aggravating energy of litigation and court cases flies to the South of homes and offices in 2010. This star brings an air of hostility and creates a variety of problems associated with arguments, fights and misunderstandings to everyone directly hit by it. In extreme cases, when this Wood element star is enhanced, the quarrelling can lead to court cases and even violence for residents spending time in the South. The number 3 star can cause a host of interpersonal strife to flare up even between the closest of allies, friends and loved ones. It causes tempers to fray and usually manifests in a great deal of impatience.

Fortunately for anyone with a bedroom in the South, the quarrelsome star 3 is less strong this year because its intrinsic Wood element is exhausted by the Fire energy of the South. The 3 Star is a Wood element star and the traditional way of overcoming this is to exhaust it with Fire element energy. Anything that suggests Fire is an excellent cure, so all kinds of lights and the color red are suitable. Hence because the South is so strongly associated with fire energy, the sector itself has its own in-built remedy!

Earth Seal in the South

A good indication for the South location (and for those born in the year of the Horse) in 2010 is that the sector benefits from the presence of the **Earth Seal** brought by the luck star of the 24 mountains. This brings good fortune to those residing in this part of the house, especially if you take action to enhance this energy with Earth element activators such as solid crystal or glass globes.

Houses that face South should place the **Fire Sword** here as a safeguard against being hauled into court or getting involved in a tiresome legal battle perhaps left over from past years. If you are already involved in a prolonged battle with someone or some company, the number 3 star will hurt you if you have a bedroom in the South or if your house is facing South.

If this is the case with you, use **strong bright lights** to help overcome it. A dramatic remedy which brings some relief from aggravation is simply to paint the South part of the house a bright red – perhaps a wall or a door if this is the front part of the home.

The Flaming Sword symbolizes Metal & Fire energy - this is one of the best remedies to subdue Star 3. Place it in the South in 2010.

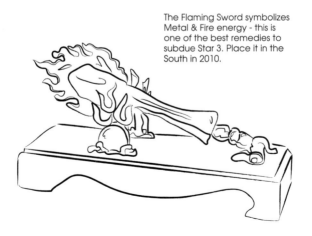

MISFORTUNE STAR 5
Hits the Southwest in 2010

SE	S	SW
7	3	(5)
6	8	1
2	4	9
NE	N	NW

(E on the left side, W on the right side)

The Five Yellow Star, flies to the SW hurting the matriarchal energy of every home. This is a serious affliction which must be suppressed with the 5 element pagoda with "Hum" empowering syllable.

The Five Yellow star, also known as the *wu wang*, flies to the SW in 2010 making it a very serious affliction this year. This is a star to be feared as it brings aggravations, misfortunes and most of all in 2010, a big weakness to the Matriarch of the family. This is because the SW is usually associated with the mother energy of any home. And in feng shui, when the matriarchal energy gets afflicted, it usually has a strong impact on the rest of the family as well. This is because SW is the source of the family's nurturing chi.

As we are currently in the period of 8, the SW/NE directional axis exerts a great deal of strong chi for any home and when the energy of this axis brings misfortune, it must be firmly subdued. In 2010, this axis direction appears to be powerfully afflicted, with Five Yellow in the SW and 2 in the NE.

> The *wu wang* is very dangerous in normal years, but in 2010, it is extremely strong as it is an earth star flying into an earth sector. Likewise the illness star 2 in the NE is also strong! The *wu wang* thus gets strengthened, as a result of which, it can create havoc for mothers and also for other older women of the household.

Those having their bedroom here will also feel its negative impact and when a house faces SW, the *wu wang* can bring bad luck which affects the entire household. If there is a door in the SW that you frequently use, the *wu wang* gets activated, and this further compounds its strength. So, it is advisable to use another door if possible. The opening and closing of doors activates the energy around it. Everyone should suppress the pernicious effects of this number 5 star – otherwise its negative influence can spread to other parts of the house. It must be curbed with metallic and symbolic remedies. These should be prominently placed on a table or sideboard in the

SW of the house and office as well as in the SW of afflicted bedrooms and living rooms.

Cures for the Wu Wang

For 2010, we are recommending three powerful cures for this affliction. These should be used together for fast and powerful results.

1) Five Element Pagoda with Ten Powerful Mantras

This year, this traditional remedy comes with a larger base and the powerful mantras are stamped all round the base of the pagoda. This version of the five element pagoda is recommended for use in larger rooms and is best when placed above ground, preferably on a table. The mantras on the pagoda transform it into a powerful object which should be respected, so place it on a table.

The Five Element Pagoda with Ten Powerful Mantras is one of the most effective cures for the *wu wang*.

2) Five Element Bell

This cure is best when 12 inches high. The bell is divided into 5 horizontal sections, each one signifying the 5 elements. The bell also has powerful mantras embossed on its outside. The remedy comes from striking of the bell. Here the sound of metal struck on metal is what will suppress the negative influences of the Five Yellow. Strike the bell at least once a day, and more often if residents are going through a hard time. The sound of the bell with the resonance of the mantras is very powerful for dispelling bad vibes. All misfortune luck gets alleviated instantly. If you prefer, you can use the ringing bell instead, and the way to suppress the *wu wang* is to ring this bell each day.

3) Double Circle Pendant

If you want to ensure continuous suppression of any ongoing misfortune luck or if you or your family are going through tough times associated with broken relationships or loss of income (such as losing your job) it is beneficial for family members to wear the double circle pendant. This will activate powerful Metal energy to exhaust the effects of the *wu wang*. Better yet if the pendant has multiple circles and in the center there is a square design. This indicates the *wu wang* is kept under control.

Please note that unless suppressed, the *wu wang* brings severe illness, accidents and loss that occur in many aspects of life. It is the catalyst for bringing all kinds of misfortune. It can cause your life to suddenly collapse around you. When you read about tragedies striking a family, you can be sure that the five yellow is somehow responsible, either because it afflicts the main door or the room the person occupies. Sometimes, just facing the *wu wang* direction can bring some kind of bad luck.

If your main door, your bedroom or even your office desk is afflicted by the *wu wang*, the affliction must be dealt with before the 4th February 2010. Do not be careless or forget about it as bad luck can manifest quickly. When it does it might be too late to do something about it. Prevention is better than cure, so do not wait until it is too late. Those living in SW facing houses should take note of the months when you need to be extra careful of the five yellow. We stress this because it is a serious feng shui affliction in 2010.

As a person born in the **Tiger Year** you must be extra careful in the month of November as this is the month when the Five Yellow also flies into your month chart. This is when you are subjected to a double whammy of bad luck so do be careful.

Misfortunes caused by the Five Yellow in 2010 can be severe business loss or threatening terminal illness. Houses that face the SW require one or all three of the remedies suggested. This is because houses that face SW are sitting NE which is being hit by the illness star. Metal energy works well here at both the front and back of the house.

If you reside in a room located in the SW, your cures should be inside your room. Make sure that the cures are in place from February 4th, the start of the Chinese solar year. While remedies used in previous years can be recycled after they have been cleansed with salt, it is better to retire them by throwing them into the sea or a fast moving river.

It is always better to use new products with fresh new energy. New remedies are better for suppressing feng shui afflictions, as the energy of new objects are more vigorous and thus more effective.

Observe the "NO RENOVATION RULE" for the Southwest in 2010

It is extremely harmful if you were to undertake any kind of knocking, banging or digging in the SW in 2010. This will especially hurt the mother of the household. So do observe the "No Renovation" rule for the SW during 2010. Any kind of demolition work poses serious danger. Misfortunes are sure to manifest. It is especially dangerous to drill floors, knock down walls, dig holes in the ground, engage in any kind of destructive work or make excessive banging kind of noise.

Any of these activities have the effect of activating the *wu wang* which in turn is sure to trigger very severe misfortune luck to suddenly manifest. The way to safeguard against this is to keep the SW location of the home very quiet in 2010.

If you really have to undertake renovations in your house and it encroaches into the SW sector, make sure your cures are in place **and** make very sure the renovation does not start or end in the SW. No one should be staying in the SW sector when renovations are going on.

If you are adding to the SW however,, and not disturbing the space with banging and digging, then that kind of renovation is acceptable; and can even be auspicious. But as long as you are demolishing or digging the earth/floor, it is advisable to postpone whatever you may be planning for the sector.

ROBBERY STAR 7
Strikes the Southeast in 2010

SE	S	SW
(7)	3	5
E 6	8	1 W
2	4	9
NE	N	NW

The Robbery Star brings violence & turmoil in your life. Protect against it with the Blue Rhino and Elephant

This is a very unwelcome affliction that is brought by the number 7. It is a number that causes political turmoil and sparks aggressive behavior that can become something serious very quickly. This is because it is the violent star. It brings out the worst in all who come under its influence or is afflicted by it.

In 2010, it flies to the SE where its presence creates dangerous situations for those residing here in the SE sector. This star number completely dominates the sector because being of the Metal element, it easily controls the Wood element of the SE. So the 7 is very lethal here.

The SE is the place of the eldest daughter so daughters should be especially careful. Anyone living in the SE should also be very careful as this star number brings danger of violence and burglary. It is advisable to try and avoid this sector.

> For 2010, because the water element is so lacking during the year, the best remedy for the SE - for the whole house to be protected from the 7 star - is to display the **Blue Rhinoceros & Elephant Water Globe**. This will be a very powerful cure for the violent burglary star. Placing or incorporating the **water globe** or **water motif** here is also an excellent idea.

The good news is that in the year 2010 the Luck Stars of the 24 mountains for the SE are extremely auspicious. Thus the *Star of the Golden Deity,* which brings heaven's blessings, benefits all those residing in the SE1 location. At the same time, the SE3 location is favored by the *Heavenly Seal* which also brings auspicious energy. This benefits anyone staying here.

These two powerful heavenly stars of the 24 mountains are an excellent buffer against the burglary star as it is sandwiched between two powerful stars. This helps residents of the SE overcome burglary woes in 2010.

In terms of feng shui, the best way to overcome its negative effect of 7 is to have a large water feature, as Water exhausts the vitality of 7.

Water is also auspicious for the SE where it strengthens the intrinsic Wood energy here. Those who already have a water feature here such as a pond in the garden or an internal water feature in the living room will be happy to know that in addition to generating good fortune luck for the eldest daughter of the family, Water here will suppress the Burglary Star and bring wonderful much needed water element energy for the year.

The Tai Sui Resides in the Northeast in 2010

The 2010 *Tai Sui* resides in the location of NE3 which is the home location of the Crouching Tiger; however, despite occupying the den of the Tiger, this year's Tai Sui is not wrathful, and like the Tai Sui of the previous year, is not quick to anger even when disturbed or confronted. Nevertheless, it is advisable to keep the Tai Sui appeased and happy. The best way of doing this is to place the Tai Sui plaque with specially written Taoist talisman. This not only appeases the Tai Sui, it also successfully enlists the Tai Sui's help to attract prosperity and abundance especially for those born in the years of the Tiger and its allies. So in 2010 the Tai Sui is generally helpful to all those born in the Year of the Tiger.

The Effect of the Tai Sui Affliction
The Chinese who believe in feng shui take the affliction of the Tai Sui very seriously as emphasized in the *Treatise on Harmonizing Times and Distinguishing Directions* compiled under the patronage of the Qianlong Emperor during his reign in the mid Eighteenth century. The Emperor placed great importance on the astrological influences on the luck of the dynasty. He stressed particularly on the correct ways for selecting times and aligning houses and went to great lengths to ensure that all knowledge on these matters were properly catalogued.

The Treatise confirms that the astrology of the Tai Sui has been recognized since mid century BCE (for over 2000 years) and states that locations where the Tai Sui resides and where the Tai Sui has just vacated are lucky locations. So note that in 2010, the locations of NE1 and NE3 are lucky. Those having their rooms in these locations will enjoy the patronage of the Tai Sui.

The Treatise explains that it is unlucky to reside in the location where the Tai Sui is progressing towards i.e. clockwise on the astrology compass and in 2010, this means the East 2 location; it is unlucky to directly confront the Tai Sui's residence. It is unlucky to 'face' the Tai Sui because this is deemed rude, so the advice for 2010 is not to directly face NE3 direction.

Actually doing so also causes you to directly confront another Tiger and this is definitely not advisable. There is an old Chinese saying which reminds us that in any mountain there can only be one Tiger! So do not confront your own location direction!

This means that you should remember not to face NE3 even if this is your most favored direction under the Eight Mansions School of Feng Shui. When you face the Tai Sui, nothing you do will go smoothly as obstacles surface unexpectedly and friends turn into adversaries. So the Tiger should not face its own home direction in 2010 and instead should have its back protected by the Tai Sui. This means facing SW3. Everyone else - all other animal signs - should follow this same advice. Be careful of this taboo if you don't want your good fortune to get blocked by the Tai Sui.

Do not face the NE3 direction!

It is very beneficial to place the beautiful **Pi Yao** in the NE as this celestial chimera is incredibly auspicious. For getting on the good side of the Tai Sui they are also effective. They also bring exceptional good fortune into the home. Get them in jade or any earth color to enhance their power in a year when Wood chi brings wealth and Earth chi brings productive resources.

Important Reminder

An important reminder for 2010 is to not disturb the place of the Tai Sui which means the NE3 location should not be renovated this year. Refrain from drilling, digging, banging and knocking down walls or digging holes in the ground. Those starting renovations in 2010 to change to a Period 8 house are advised not to start or end their renovations in NE3 and to avoid starting or ending their renovations in November when the direction of the Tai Sui is afflicted by misfortune star of *wu wang*.

Do not start or end renovations in the NE this year.

The Three Killings
Flies to the North in 2010

In 2010 the North of every building is afflicted by the three killings. This feng shui aggravation affects only the primary directions, but that means its bad effects are felt over a larger area of the house – 90 degrees!

This affliction brings three severe misfortunes associated with loss, grief and sadness. Its location each year is charted according to the animal sign that rules the year. Thus it flies to the North in 2010 because the Tiger belongs to the Triangle of Affinity made up of the Tiger, Dog and Horse, and of these three animal signs it is the Horse which occupies a cardinal direction (South).

The Three Killings is thus in the North, the direction that is directly opposite the Horse.

The Three Killings cause three kinds of loss, the loss of one's good reputation, the loss of a loved one and the loss of wealth. When you suffer a sudden reversal of fortune, it is usually due to being hit by the three killings. In 2010, the three killings reside in the North where it poses some danger to the middle sons of the family. Anyone occupying the North is vulnerable to being hit by the three killings.

Cures for the Three Killings

In terms of cures, we recommend the three divine guardians comprising the Chi Lin, the Fu Dog and the Pi Yao. We have been using these celestial protectors with great success for several years now and we can continue using them for 2010. It is however advisable to bring in newly minted ones to ensure their energy is fresh and there is strong vigor and vitality.

The Three Divine Guardians can be used to control the Three Killings affliction in the North in 2010.

The three guardians are a great favorite with the Chinese and they create a powerful and invisible shield of protective energy that prevents the Three Killings from passing into the home or office. It is a good idea to keep all North sector doors and windows closed during the afternoon hours as this is an effective way of preventing the energy of the Three Killings from entering.

Another powerful set of cures to overpower the Three Killings in the Year of the Tiger are the three deities each sitting on a Tiger and therefore symbolizing their dominance over this powerful beast. Deities that sit on the Tiger are usually also wealth-bringing Gods. The most effective is to line up the Wealth God sitting on a Tiger (Tsai Shen Yeh), the Eight Immortal sitting on a Tiger and one of the 18 Arhats sitting on a Tiger. If you prefer, you can also display just one of them. The symbolism of these three powerful Deities cannot be matched and their presence in the home is also an effective way of avoiding all the difficult luck brought by the Tiger in 2010.

A Wealth God sitting on a tiger symbolizes his dominance over the animal and displaying his image in the home helps you bring the fierce energies of the Tiger Year under control.

THE LUCKY STAR 4 bringing
Romance & Study Luck to the North

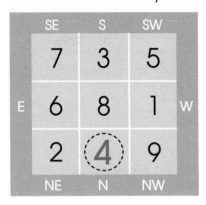

SE	S	SW
7	3	5
6	8	1
2	(4)	9
NE	N	NW

The lucky Star 4 flies North bringing love & romance this part of houses in 2010. The star 4 is also beneficial for anyone engaged in writing, study and work.

The North comes out of a challenging year to play host to the romance-bringing star in 2010. Last year, the North had been afflicted by the *wu wang*, but this year this is the location which attracts love and marriage opportunities, and developments of the heart brought by the peach blossom vibes here.

This luck is considered good for singles and unmarried people but is viewed with suspicion for those who are already married. *Peach blossom luck* is usually linked to temptations of the heart and to unfaithful behavior for the older married. As such, this is not a star favored by those already married. So if your room is in the North part of the house and you are already married, it is not a bad idea to symbolically suppress it with bright lights or Fire element energy. This should prevent either husband or wife succumbing to temptation coming their way. Placing an **amethyst geode** tied with red string and attached to the bed is a Taoist way of keeping the marriage stable, and spouses faithful.

Unmarried people who want to activate their marriage luck can do so with the presence of all the marriage symbols such as the **dragon and phoenix**, and the **double happiness** character. Here in the North, the romance star favors young men who are still single. So those of you keen on enhancing marriage luck should activate your peach blossom luck by placing a **bejeweled Rat** in the North. However, do note that the Chinese usually do not favor romance blossoming in the Year of the Tiger and usually prefer to wait until the following year of the Rabbit before committing themselves in a new love relationship.

The double happiness symbol is ideal for attracting marriage luck. It should be worn or incorporated into house or room decor for best results.

Scholastic Luck

Those residing in the North will also enjoy the other influences brought by the same number 4 star which are related to scholastic and literary pursuits. The number 4's literary side is strong bringing academic luck to those residing in this part of the home. Those facing North will also benefit from this powerful star of learning and is especially suitable for students and those sitting for examinations.

> The direction North stands for career luck, so this auspicious number is a very positive star here. The only problem will be that love can be a distraction, so if you want to enhance the scholastic side of this star, you should place literary symbols here.

The number 4 benefits those engaged in writing and literary careers. Those employed in a writing career or in the media or involved in any kind of academic pursuits benefit from staying in the North. Enhancing this part of the home is sure to bring benefits.

Feng shui energizers for the North in 2010 are categorized into those benefiting the romance side and those wanting to activate the scholastic side. For love and romance, place **mandarin ducks** here or better yet, hang a **love mirror** to reflect in the energies of the cosmic universe from outside. Meanwhile, those wanting to jumpstart their scholastic or literary pursuits should look for a good specimen of a **single-pointed quartz crystal** and then write a powerful wishfulfilling mantra on it. This is an excellent way of helping you to improve your concentration and your studies.

WHITE STAR 1 brings
Triumphant Success to the West

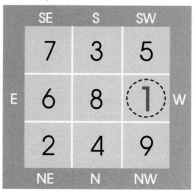

SE	S	SW
7	3	5

E			W
6	8	(1)	

2	4	9
NE	N	NW

The Victory Star is in the West. It is flanked by the 2 "Big Auspicious" stars indication of the 24 mountains. This makes the West sector extremely lucky in 2010 and those having rooms here can take advantage of this.

Those residing in rooms in the West will benefit from the white star of victory, the number 1 star, which brings triumph and success in 2010. This star number helps you to win in any competitive situation. The attainment of success is easier for you, if you energize the number 1 star correctly and effectively.

The Victory Banner is a symbol of winning over the competition. Excellent for those in the running for a promotion.

In 2010, this star brings good fortune to **young women**, especially the youngest daughters of families and also the youngest women in any household. However, please note that the number 1 star in 2010 is not as vigorous as it was last year. There is definitely a relative reduction in energy. Anyone residing in this part of the house will benefit from wearing the **Victory Banner**. It is important that this be made of gold or metal to strengthen the Metal element of this corner.

CELESTIAL STAR 6
Creates Windfall Luck in the East

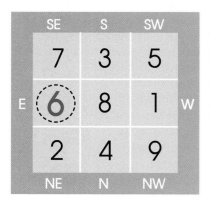

The celestial 6 brings excellent news through the year. The number 6 stands for heavenly energy which unites with earth and mankind to create the trinity of Tien Ti Ren.

This is the number 6 white star associated with the powerful Trigram *Chien*, so its presence in the East creates synergy luck between father and eldest son. **When the bedroom of the family's eldest son is located in this sector of the house, he is certain to benefit very much from unexpected good fortune,** the kind that comes without warning, and is thus a welcome surprise. The 6 Star brings heaven's celestial blessings.

In Flying Star feng shui, the number 6 signifies everything to do with the management of economics and finances. At its peak, 6 stands for authority, influence and control over money, like being the Head of the Federal Reserve Board. When 6 appears in the East it suggests economic power does well in the hands of a **young man**. This is also a Military Star which brings promotions and mentor luck.

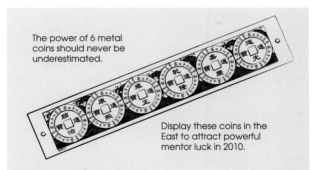

The power of 6 metal coins should never be underestimated.

Display these coins in the East to attract powerful mentor luck in 2010.

6 Metal Coins

It is incredibly beneficial to activate this auspicious star to benefit the whole household and this can be done by displaying **6 Large Smooth Coins** in the East. Doing so will ensure that everything will move smoothly. It is also a good way of attracting Mentor Luck to the household - powerful and influential friends who will assist you and open doorways to opportunities for you.

Updating Feng Shui

Updating feng shui is something that many wealthy and powerful families living in places like Hong Kong, Taiwan and now China arrange for without fail, each year. In recent years, the practice is also becoming increasingly popular in places like Singapore, Malaysia and Indonesia. Today, families consult feng shui retainers who use their expertise to insure homes against the intangible feng shui afflictions of the year.

These days anyone keen to do so can update their feng shui. At *World of Feng Shui*, the annual feng shui chart is analyzed each year. this make sit possible for us to understand the nature and location of bad luck afflictions and good luck indications.

We explain the use of different remedies each year through our popular Feng Shui Extravaganzas which are live whole day events held in Singapore, East & West and Malaysia, the United States, the UK and in 2010, for the first time, also in French Polynesia! These events go a very long way towards protecting them against the year's afflictions.

The *Feng Shui Extravaganza* road show takes place over 5 weekends before the lunar New Year, and is a wonderful way to connect with feng shui enthusiasts and to explain the fine points on what needs to be done each New Year.

We genuinely look forward to doing these road shows. Those interested in attending any of our 2010 Extravaganzas, please note they are held in January and February 2010 and the dates and venues can be accessed at *www.wofs.com*.

Part 5
Improving personal feng shui

Each New Year, in addition to updating your space feng shui, it also benefits to make some adjustments that update your personal feng shui too.

The practice of personalised feng shui takes into account of your animal sign as well as your individual Kua number.

You need to make adjustments to your facing directions and sitting locations to accomodate the different energies of the Tiger Year; thus your lucky and unlucky directions as indicated by your Kua number must be fine-tuned to counter of the year's afflictions.

Remember that in using your lucky directions, you must always be mindfully aware of the influences of various annual afflictions. Even when a direction is generally very "lucky" for you, if in the Year of the Tiger that direction is negatively affected in any way, then you must NOT face that direction. Annual energies usually override Kua number lucky directions. Thus if your love direction is afflicted this year, then it is best not to activate romance luck this year.

Personalizing your feng shui makes a big difference to improving luck especially in a year as challenging as the Tiger Year 2010. Using your birth Lo Shu number to see how it combines with this year's Lo Shu number 8 also offers some interesting feng shui nuances for you to work with.

Finetuning Your Kua Lucky & Unlucky Directions

The compass based method of using your Kua number to determine if you are an East or a West group person, and also for finding out your lucky and unlucky directions, is one of the easiest ways to practice and benefit from compass formula feng shui. Once you know your lucky directions, all you need to do is to arrange your home and office

Lo Shu & Kua Numbers of the Tiger

Birth Year	Element Tiger	Age in 2010	Lo Shu No. at Birth	KUA No. for Men	KUA No. for Women
1938	Earth Tiger	72	8	8	7
1950	Metal Tiger	60	5	5	1
1962	Water Tiger	48	2	2	4
1974	Wood Tiger	36	8	8	7
1986	Fire Tiger	24	5	5	1
1998	Earth Tiger	12	2	2	4

and the furniture within, in a way which enables you to always face at least one of your good luck (and unafflicted) directions. Just doing this will immediately make a difference to your luck for the year. The formula in detail also identifies 4 different kinds of good luck and 4 severities of bad luck, with each being represented by a compass direction.

The 4 good directions for instance allows you to choose whether to face a direction that brings you

success, love, good health or personal growth.
The formula also identifies four kinds of misfortune
directions, describing the nature and intensity of each
of these bad luck directions. Once you are aware of
your misfortune directions, systematically change
your sitting and sleeping arrangements so you never
face or have your head pointed to any of the bad luck
directions. Feng shui is really that simple!

But there is one extra thing you need to take account
of and that is to finetune these lucky and unlucky
directions each year. Here are three things you must
do at the start of each new year:

1) Check if any of your lucky directions are afflicted
by any of the afflictive stars of the New Year. This
requires you to study the afflicted directions laid out
in the previous chapter.

2) Take note of your own animal sign compass
location and ensure it is properly activated and
kept free of clutter, even if this is not one of your
lucky directions. Remember that your animal sign
direction is more important and also over rides the
Kua directions! Your animal sign direction (which
in the case of the Tiger is NE3), is always lucky for
you irrespective of what the Kua formula indicates.
It overrides the Kua formula but if the direction is

afflicted by a bad number star for the year, then the location and direction should be avoided. In the year of the Tiger, the NE is afflicted by the illness star 2 so to be on the safe side it is better for the West group Tiger born men with Kua number 2, 5 and 8 and the Tiger lady whose Kua is 7 not to face the NE or sleep with head pointed to the NE. Even if NE is lucky for you, it is definitely not advisable to use this direction in 2010.

As for Tiger ladies with Kua numbers 1 and 4, you are East group people so the NE has a double whammy effect for you. It brings five ghosts i.e. troublemakers to those with Kua number 1, and total loss for those with Kua 4. In 2010, the Tiger does not have much luck in terms of this particular formula.

3) Look at your Lo Shu number at birth and see how this interacts with the Lo Shu number of the year which is 8. The Lo Shu numbers of Tigers are either 2, 5 or 8, all of which are Earth numbers. Find out whether any of your lucky directions are in any way affected by bad luck stars during the year. Every year, the direction of misfortune-bringing afflictions change location, so it is vital to make sure that any lucky direction you may be facing is NOT afflicted in 2010.

Lucky & Unlucky Directions for Tiger

Male/Female Tigers	Male	Male	Male	Female	Female	Female
Kua Number	2	5	8	1	4	7
Success Direction	NE*	NE*	SW*	SE*	North	NW
Love Direction	NW	NW	West	South*	East	NE*
Health Direction	West	West	NW	East	South*	SW*
Personal Growth	SW*	SW*	NE	North	SE*	West
Bad Luck Direction	East	East	South*	West	NW	North
Five Ghosts Direction	SE*	SE*	North	NE*	SW	South*
Six Killings Direction	South*	South*	East	NW	West	SE*
Total Loss Directions	North	North	SE*	SW*	NE*	East

Note: All directions that are afflicted in 2010 are marked with *. When a direction that is lucky for you is afflicted, you are recommended not to use that direction for the year. When the direction afflicted is one of your bad luck directions, then you must be extra certain you do not get hurt by either facing this direction or occupying this location in your home or office.

This is because time-sensitive annual afflictions exert greater strength than personalized directions. Indeed, annual energy flow usually possesses greater impact even than Period energies. Time dimension feng shui affects the luck of the world more strongly than the space dimension of feng shui. Only when you practice your feng shui with this particular awareness, will you get the most out of feng shui.

To Activate Success Luck

Your personalized Success direction is your *sheng chi* direction. If you can face your success direction without being afflicted in any way by the annual afflictions then success luck flows smoothly, bringing advancement, growth and enhanced stature in your professional life. But you MUST make sure your Success direction is not afflicted.

Look at your Success direction for those born in the Tiger Year summarized in the table above and you can systematically investigate which are the directions that are absolutely taboo for you. These mean your own bad luck directions as well as your good luck directions that are afflicted. Facing either of these directions will have an adverse effect on your success luck.

For 2010, the *sheng chi* direction of all Male Tigers is afflicted by the illness or *wu wang* stars which bring sickness and misfortune; of the two, the SW *sheng chi* is the more badly affected. Thus for gentlemen Tigers with Kua 8, and especially the 36 year old Water Tiger, it is better you give the SW a pass this year and face West instead. Note that the direction West has very auspicious energy this year. West is flanked on both sides by the stars of big auspicious, and West is also your good relationship direction.

Success Luck for the Tiger Born

Kua Number	1	4	7	2	5	8
Male/ Female	Female	Female	Female	Male	Male	Male
Success Direction	SE*	North	NW	NE*	NE	SW*

If you have no choice and cannot change your facing direction at work even when the direction is afflicted, then you should assess whether it is your Success direction that is being hurt and if so, how strong the affliction is.

In this case, we have seen that the gentlemen Tigers with their 2 or 8 Kua numbers have their success direction afflicted! So for you, if you have no choice but to face these afflicted directions, then those facing SW must place the **five element pagoda** in front of them and wear the **five element pagoda pendant**; while those facing the NE should use the **wu lou symbol** or the **Antakharana** symbol.

As for Lady Tigers, the 60 year old Metal Lady Tiger and the 24 year old Fire Lady Tiger have their *sheng chi* direction of **SE** afflicted by the violent star 7. You should either avoid facing SE altogether in 2010, otherwise whatever success you achieve will be taken away from you; or you should place a **blue Rhino/ Elephant** in front of you on your desk, and also carry one with you at all times.

Those of you facing North will also be facing the *three killings* and this is fine, and is in fact very beneficial, except that it is a good idea to place the three celestial guardians on your desk as an additional safeguard.

The Wood Lady Tiger whose *sheng chi* is NW can face the NW *sheng chi* direction without worrying about afflictions. On balance you can see that Tiger is having a hard time in 2010 as the year is full of minefields that directly impede your success luck! With the cures in place however, the effect of the afflictions will not be so bad.

Kua Number 1

Lady Tigers with Kua number 1 belong to the East group and for them, their Success direction is afflicted by the violent burglary star. This indicates that if you face your Success direction in 2010, success will be robbed from under your nose. There is betrayal that affects your chances of moving upward professionally. This year you must not allow other matters to distract you, otherwise bad people who want what you have could succeed in politicking against you. The 60 year old Metal Tiger lady as well as the 23 year old Fire Tiger lady in particular must make sure not to face SE even though this is your *sheng chi*.

Note that Success luck in feng shui means that professional and working life going smoothly. When obstacles manifest, you can overcome them, and when troublesome people cause trouble for you, you can defeat them.

Kua Number 4

The lady Tiger with Kua number 4 has North as their Success direction. This brings literary success luck for the 48 year old Water Tiger lady and also helps it to activate the water element. This really brings excellent luck in 2010. It allows you to activate your *sheng chi* direction and also energizes it with water, as North is the place of Water.

Furthermore, with the Three Killings direction there, directly staring down this affliction is an effective way of keeping this afflictive star under control. So facing North brings you success. But do remember to strenuously avoid sitting in or facing the NE and SW compass directions.

Note that both NE and SW are seriously afflicted in 2010 and cures must be placed there.

Kua Number 7

The 36 year old Fire Lady Tiger with Kua 7 belongs to the West group and for you, your Success direction is NW which in 2010 is auspicious as it signifies future prosperity. There is a hidden threat of robbery afflicting this direction brought by the 24 mountain star but this is easily taken care of by placing a **blue Rhino** in the NW. Generally however, if you face the NW direction and you are also the main wage earner of the house, the direction is sure to serve you well this year.

Just to make sure you are not affected by those who might want to wish you harm keep the energy of your Five Ghost direction i.e. South, strongly subdued. The South suffers from the quarrelsome star of 3 which brings heavy politicking and misunderstandings. Even when you walk away from trouble, others might find reason to stir up trouble against you. So simply avoiding facing the South is not enough, you must also place the remedy against the 3 star in the South.

Get the powerful **Magic Fire Wheel** here to make sure no one with bad intentions can harm you. Note that the **fire sword cure** for the 3 star is not strong enough if this direction is also your 5 ghosts direction because the element of Five Ghosts is also Fire. To overcome the Five Ghosts, you need the *magic fire wheel* surrounded by a ring of fire! This is the correct symbol to overcome the five ghosts (bad people) affliction as the wheel made of eight metal spokes is strong enough to keep the five ghosts properly subdued. This is even more important if you are in politics!

Kua Numbers 2 & 5

All men born in a Tiger Year belong to the West group, so they tend to benefit more from Period 8 than their female counterparts.

In 2010 however, Tiger males have fewer opportunities as all three of their Kua numbers, 2, 5 and 8 seem to have afflicted directions as their *sheng chi*. The gentleman with Kua number 2 is the 48 year old Metal Tiger and the 12 year old Fire Tiger teenager. The Tiger with Kua 5 follows the lucky and unlucky directions of Kua 2, so NE is also its *sheng chi*.

However the 60 year old Earth Tiger and the 23 year old Wood Tiger should note that since your Kua is 5, the Five Yellow is not necessarily your enemy. Indeed those with Kua 5 usually enjoy indirect good fortune (usually brought by bad people) when the 5 flies into their location, so although you cannot face the NE, you can face the SW despite the Five Yellow being there. You will not only be able to subdue this affliction, you might even benefit from it!

But in facing the NE, you can fall victim to the illness star. This means that if you use this direction as an aid to attracting success luck, then whatever success comes your way comes at a cost to your health. Better to avoid this direction and let the year pass.

Kua Numbers 8

The male Tiger with Kua 8 is the 36 year old Water Tiger who belongs to the West group. For you, SW is your Success direction and while this is excellent for Period 8, in this particular year 2010, the SW is afflicted by the *wu wang,* which is a very serious affliction.

The *wu wang* will definitely cause you problems and it is better not to face the SW in 2010, as doing so brings a host of obstacles rather than success. It is better to face the NW as this is the direction that has no negative connotations. You can also face West as this brings victory in competitive situations.

The West is very auspicious in 2010!

Meanwhile, take note that your *Five Ghosts* direction is North and unhappily for you, the **Three Killings affliction** is also there in 2010. This direction is the source of people problems for you. Gossip and trouble may cause you stress unless you ensure the Three Killings are kept suppressed with the **three celestials**. Also place the cure against the Five Ghosts – the **magic fire wheel** – here in the North. Finally, make sure you do not face North or sit in the North, otherwise troublesome people are sure to cause you a lot of problems.

To Maintain Good Health

These days, with international travel being so extensive and people around the world on the move so much, there is always the real danger of epidemics spreading across continents. Good health can no longer be taken for granted and it is now advisable not only to keep the energy of the home vibrant and clean, you must also make certain that where you live is always filled with a good supply of yang energy.

It is when chi energy is moving and not stagnating that residents within enjoy good health. A healthy home is where residents enjoy good resistance against germs and are not in danger of picking up infectious disease. Thus good health in feng shui terms means you should eat well and auspiciously; and also live well with enough exercise and with no mental stress. When you have a good healthy environment you are unlikely to be vulnerable to illness.

Health Directions for Tigers

Kua Number	1	4	7	2	5	8
Male/ Female	Female	Female	Female	Male	Male	Male
Health Direction	East	South*	SW*	West	West	NW
Bad Luck Direction	West	NW	North	East	East	South*
6 Killings Direction	NW	West	SE*	South*	South*	East

Sickness in any home is almost always due to bad feng shui and also because the house itself is affected by illness star vibrations which are left unchecked AND thus flourish because the environment within fosters it. When someone gets sick in any household, the sickness energy is always infectious so residents will get sick, one by one.

Apart from catching the bug from each other, this is also due to the illness star getting activated; and then it affects everyone irrespective of which part of the house you stay in. Afflictive star influences can move from one part of the house to another if they are not strongly curbed at source. This means placing the metal cures and the **wu lou** in the **NE corner** which this year is the source of illness vibes.

> For those who want to capture your individual good health direction, you can sleep with your head pointed to your Health direction. This is said to be the direction of the *Heavenly Doctor*.

The table to the left shows the good health luck directions for all those born in the years of the Tiger.

Note that all male Tigers have no problems with their health direction in 2010 and they can use their good health direction to recover from illness; but lady Tigers with Kua numbers 4 and 7 have afflicted directions in 2010. Thus those with Kua number 4 have South as their *tien yi* direction and in 2010 this is of the quarrelsome 3 star which is super bad for mental health, so it is advisable not to face South if you are ill. Those with Kua 7 have **SW** as their health direction and here the affliction is the *wu wang* which is a very serious affliction.

Becoming a Star at School

For the 12 year old Earth Tiger child, 2010 brings little in the way of success luck and even less good health energy so the potential for you to emerge as a sports star this year don't look so good. But what 2010 brings is a good dose of inner confidence and a greater self assurance which is enough to propel you towards working out a plan for long term success. What you need to do to harness good luck is to make sure you sit facing your *Personal Growth* direction when you are studying at home, working on an assignment, doing your homework or sitting for an examination.

For the boy, your best direction is SW, but unfortunately in 2010, the SW is afflicted by the *wu wang* so the advice is for you to sit facing NW which will help you lay the groundwork for the future, and also the West which is very auspicious in 2010. Get yourself a a good compass and try to face either NW or West when you are studying or working.

For the girl, your *Personal Growth* direction is SE which is also afflicted in 2010 so this is not a good year to sit facing the SE. Here the violent star 7 is lurking, bringing cheating luck, so sit facing North instead. The North is Water, which helps you benefit from this all important element in 2010. But more significantly, the North in 2010 houses the literary star, so this benefits those of you still at school. North is also your success direction, so for 2010, this is the direction for you!

Attracting Romance

If you are looking for marriage opportunities, you must be careful that you do not meet up with married people pretending to be single. Be extra careful because the *flower of external romance* star is running amok in the Year of the Tiger. This means the libido of married people, especially married men, are at a high. Singles should thus be extra skeptical of new people coming into their lives, especially if they are actively using love rituals to attract romantic opportunities into their lives.

Here are three ways to attract love:

1) First, you can activate your personalized peach blossom luck. For the Tiger, your peach blossom animal is the Rabbit. You should place a beautiful, expensive looking Rabbit in the East location of your bedroom. The Rabbit is considered as a very sexy

creature in feng shui, bringing also the luck of family, so do look for a beautiful white Rabbit to attract a good romantic partner! Do not get a "Rabbit" from pavement stalls and flea markets where the energy they are absorbing is unlikely to be very good! Also make certain they are not cracked or chipped.

2) The peach blossom star lands in the North in 2010. This is a powerful love direction for activating marriage luck. So no matter your age, irrespective of whether you have been married before, this is the direction to activate as well if you wish to benefit from the year's romantic energies.

3) Most effective of all is that you should sleep with your head pointed to your *nien yen* direction. This is shown below for the Tiger men and women.

Nien Yen Direction for the Tiger

Kua Number	1	4	7	2	5	8
Male/ Female	Female	Female	Female	Male	Male	Male
Love Direction	South*	East	NE*	NW	NW	West

Sleeping with your head pointed to your love direction is the best way of attracting marriage luck; this will encourage *nien yen* vibrations to enter into your crown chakra while you sleep; but once again, do make certain that your *nien yen* direction is not afflicted during the year. The conventional advice for those wanting romance is to arrange your bed such that your head points to your *nien yen* direction when you sleep.

Based on this, it appears that those of you lady Tigers with Kua 1 and 7 have afflicted *nien yen* directions which are better not to activate. Male Tigers have no problems in their love lives this year and should they want to find love opportunities or if they are married and want children, then they should try to sleep with their heads pointed to their *nien yen* direction as shown. Both the NW and West are auspicious directions.

Interacting with Annual Lo Shu Number 8

While the feng shui chart of the year reveals the energy pattern of the year, bringing new energies to every house, the new energies also interact with your personal Lo Shu charts. This is not to be confused with the Kua numbers discussed earlier. Every animal sign is influenced by three Lo Shu charts which are created using their birth Lo Shu numbers. These numbers apply to both men and women.

The table on the following page reveals the Lo Shu number of those born in Tiger years extracted from the Thousand Year calendar. Take note that the Tiger's Lo Shu numbers are 2, 5 or 8 which reflects a number from each Lower, Middle and Upper period in the feng shui cycle of three periods which covers 180 years.

Lo Shu Numbers for the Tiger

Birth Year	Element Tiger	Age in 2010	Lo Shu No. at Birth
1938	Earth Tiger	72	8
1950	Metal Tiger	60	5
1962	Water Tiger	48	2
1972	Wood Tiger	36	8
1982	Fire Tiger	24	5
1998	Earth Tiger	12	2

The Lo Shu number at birth offers clues to the personality traits of the Tiger and how the number interacts with the current year's Lo Shu number also offers recommendations to improve the year's feng shui luck for the Tiger.

Tiger with Birth Lo Shu of 8
(affecting the 36 and 72 year old Tiger)

SE	S	SW
7	3	5
E 6	8	1 W
2	4	9
NE	N	NW

This is the Lo Shu chart for 36 and 72 year old Tigers.

The number 8 is the luckiest number of the current Period of 8 and is also the strongest. It stands for current prosperity and when considered in the light of this year's Lo Shu number of 8, we see its strength seriously strengthened. This means that those of you born in years with Lo Shu 8 will enjoy excellent opportunities in 2010. Tigers born under the Lo Shu of 8 are usually kind hearted and soft inside, so this is a Tiger with a heart of gold. He/she is also witty and endowed with excellent memory power. If you have a mole or some kind of birthmark on the right side of your cheek, your hip or your leg, you are destined to have a very easy going life. In 2010, you must light up the centre of your home, enhancing Fire energy here; and in your North or at the entrance of your house, activate with a Water feature. Using these enhancers will bring exceptional opportunities to this Tiger!

Tiger with Birth Lo Shu of 5
(affecting the 24 and 60 year old Tiger)

SE	S	SW
4	9	2
3 (E)	5	7 (W)
8	1	6
NE	N	NW

This is the Lo Shu chart for the 24 and 60 year old year old Tigers.

The number 5 is a very special number in Chinese Astrology as it is the number that bridges the low numbers with the high. The number 5 is also the centre number of the original Lo Shu grid. Tigers born with this Lo Shu number have a store of knowledge and are described as being "rich with wisdom". They are very spiritual, possessing strong faith in their religion. They are smart, quick-thinking and witty. For male Tigers, they are also influenced by the Lo Shu number of 2, while female Tigers are influenced by the number of 8. In 2010, the number 5 belongs to the trinity of Earth with the year's number 8, so you can also indirectly benefit from the number 8. Activate the centre of the home with Fire energy and the entrance in to the home with Water. This will improve your luck very much.

Tiger with Birth Lo Shu of 2
(affecting the 12 and 48 year old Tiger)

	SE	S	SW	
	1	6	8	
E	9	2	4	W
	5	7	3	
	NE	N	NW	

This is the Lo Shu chart for the 12 and 48 year old year old Tigers.

Tigers born under the Lo Shu number of 2 are extremely charming people. You have a way with words that makes you enticing and persuasive. Your life improves as you get older and in your early years, you do not feel close to your parents. The number 2 is enhanced by the number 8 as together they make up the sum-of-ten – an auspicious combination which attracts a special kind of good fortune.

The number 2 brings good health to the 12 year old, but is dangerous for the 48 year old Tiger. Take good care of your health in 2010. It is extremely beneficial to make a donation to an old folks home, hospital or any kind of charity as this will help you cross into good health.

Safeguarding Tiger's Location in 2010

Use a compass to determine the Tiger direction of your home which is NE3. This refers to the NE sector of the whole house and the NE corner of rooms you frequently use, such as your bedroom or your home office.

You should make sure the toilet, store room and kitchen of the house are NOT located in the NE. This will create a serious feng shui problem for you.

A toilet in your Tiger direction flushes away all the luck of residents belonging to the Tiger sign. Career luck is hard hit and recognition will be blocked. Those in business face an array of problems including financial loss.

A store room here locks up all your good luck. You will find it hard to fly and ambitions will get stalled. A kitchen here suppresses all your good luck and burns the wisdom arising luck.

If you envisage staying in the same home for several more years, it is advisable to consider changing the room usage of your NE sector. When you create an active space where most of your productive work gets done, it energizes your most personally important sector of the home, thereby benefiting you. Always make sure the energy here is vibrant and active, is yang in nature and never has a chance to get stale or for yin chi to accumulate. Changing the usage of the room is thus beneficial.

The Illness Star 2

In 2010, the whole NE is afflicted by the Illness Star 2 which brings sickness energies and health problems. You should thus examine whether the affliction in this part of your house or in this corner of your important rooms is made worse by the presence crystals and other earth element objects as this will strengthen the illness star considerably. Misfortune luck associated with illness can be tragic, so it is vital to keep the illness star properly and adequately subdued.

The best thing to do is place Metal energy in the NE as this will exhaust the Earth energy of the illness star. Another great idea is to place a **Medicine Buddha** image here as this brings in a celestial remedy that is spiritually powerful as well.

The feng shui remedies that suppress the Illness Star 2 are best placed in the NE of every room. This affliction affects everyone who stays in the NE room, but illness to Tiger people can be quite severe if they are unlucky enough to catch it. So here prevention is better than cure.

Improving your Door Feng Shui

One of the best ways of improving your feng shui in any year is to ensure that the **doors** you use daily into the house, into your bedroom and into your office are auspicious for you. To determine the best direction to use we always look at the four auspicious directions using the Kua formula of directions.

Improving Door Feng Shui for the Tiger

KUA Number	2 Male	5 Male	8 Male	1 Female	4 Female	7 Female
Best Door Direction Based On Sheng Chi Direction	NE	NE	SW	SE	North	NW
Best Door Facing Direction In 2010	NW	NW	West	North	North	NW

You can check the tables in this book for all your lucky directions, but what we have done is to summarize the best door facing directions for you based on your *sheng chi* direction and we have also given you our advice on best directions for each of you in 2010. We are suggesting alternatives for those whose *sheng chi* direction is afflicted.

Use a compass to determine the facing direction that works best for you, and try to use only doors that are lucky for you in any year. Be very mindful about the doors you walk under each day and update this each year. This means checking for afflictions to your doors.

For 2010, all doors that either face, or are located in the SW, NE, South, North and SE are afflicted and will respond positively to antidote remedies. Here is the list of the correct remedies which you can place either above the door, or flanking it. The more frequently you use the door, the more important it is to place these remedies. The doors referred to also include doors inside the home. These remedies do not send out harmful chi the way the Pa Kua symbol with yin arrangement of trigrams do. In the past, these were the only "cure" known and sold and many used them indiscriminately, without realizing the potential harm they can cause.

The remedies recommended here can easily correct and subdue afflictions without creating bad chi. This is a very important aspect of cures. For all main doors going into the home, it is an excellent idea to place the **powerful mantra plaques** done in red, because the mantras not only keep all bad vibes out of the house, they also bless everyone who walks under them. This is the best way to practice feng shui – to make sure it benefits you without harming others!

- **For doors facing Southwest**
  place the **five element plaque** above the door.
- **For doors facing Northeast**
  place the **wu lou door hanging** by the side of the door.

- **For doors facing South**
  place the **kalachakra mantra plaque** above the door.
- **For doors facing North**
  place the **three celestial guardians** flanking the door.
- **For doors facing Southeast**
  place **blue Rhino/Elephant door hangings** flanking the door.

Use a good reliable compass to determine your facing direction of all your doors and make sure you stand just in front of the door to determine this. Do note that even when the "door" you use to enter the house is from the garage, and it is only a small side door, it is still very important. In fact, the more you use a door, the more important it becomes.

Special Enhancers & Amulets for 2010

To ensure stability of luck for your household it is an excellent idea to activate the center of the home, or at least the center of your living room area with **a crystal globe containing blue colored water**. We have designed a very special globe in two sizes – a three inch diameter globe and a six inch diameter globe that is embossed on the outside with the 12 animal signs of the Zodiac. The globe is an excellent enhancer for the center number of 8 because this is an Earth number.

The Earth element also signifies wealth luck in 2010, so the presence of a crystal globe here is very auspicious. It is beneficial to twirl the globe daily to imbue it with yang energy. The water inside symbolically brings much needed Water element into the living area. This is because the paht chee chart tells us that Water is terribly lacking in 2010. Note that to Taoist masters, even a single drop of water can represent an entire ocean; hence water enhancers are so good for 2010!

For the Tiger person, it is an excellent idea to place an Tiger image next to the globe, letting it face NE. This creates good energy for your particular animal sign and should you so wish, you can also place your secret friend the Boar, as well as your allies, the Horse and the Dog images here as well. This will create excellent friendship energy bringing harmony and balance into your life. Special note for Tiger – please note that your ally the Horse enjoys good luck this year, so stick close to this ally!

Special Talismans for the Tiger

In 2010, the Tiger person benefits from the following cures and talismans:

• A **Metal Wu Lou** to subdue the illness star of 2010. The Tiger is afflicted by the number 2 star this year and hence vulnerable to physical and health ailments so it is good to wear protection. This is particularly important in the months of February, May, July and December.

Metal Wu Lou

Even better if you get the **Dragon and Tiger Wu Lou,** which has been specially designed to encounter the illness star faced by the Tiger person. The combination of Tiger and Dragon gives the Tiger strength. This is the Crouching Tiger Hidden Dragon scenario.

• Wear the **Antahkarana ring**, another powerful antidote to overcome the illness star. This symbol will also give you a boost in energy, allowing you the stamina and determination to finish whatever it is you are working on.

• The **Tai Sui Plaque** to appease the Grand Duke Jupiter and to bring good luck. This plaque has been designed with Tai Sui at the top, with the Pi Yao talisman at the bottom to overcome the Tai Sui. Hang above your main door, or doors you use frequently in the home. This plaque brings good energy to the home and will also protect againt intruders and people with bad intentions entering your home.

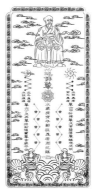

Tai Sui Plaque

• Get the **Precious Ring Talisman** to enhance your good luck this year. This powerful ring talisman, the implement carried by the Tiger-taming Arhat named Pindola, is said to possess magical powers. Hang the ring in the NE corner of your living room or office, or you can carry it with you at all times as a bag hanging. This talisman will help you channel your own Tiger powers this year in order that you may use them wisely and beneficially. It will give you greater influence with others, and boost your strategic thinking.

• Wear the **Double Wu Lou with Infinity** pendant for blessings of good health through the year. Together with the infinity symbol, this brings everlasting good health and generates a strong, healthy life, both physical and mental.

• Keep an image of the **Dragon** near you at all times. The Dragon completes the Seasonal Trinity of Spring with the Tiger and Rabbit this year, making up for the lack of a lap chun. This ensures any good luck due to you can indeed materialize.

The 24 Mountains in 2010

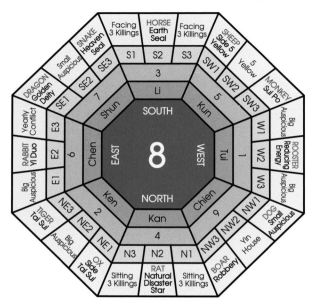

The number 8 dominates the year 2010 bringing auspicious energy to the Tiger Year. The 12 animals signs play host to the stars of the 24 mountains. These indicate the kind of cosmic forces influencing the luck for the year.

WANT TO LEARN MORE?

Don't Stop Now!

We hope you enjoyed reading your own personal horoscope book from Lillian Too & Jennifer Too. You are probably already feeling a difference in your life and enjoying the results of actions you have taken!

So, What's Next?

LILLIAN TOO'S FREE
Online Weekly Ezine NEW!

It's FREE! The latest weekly news and Feng Shui updates from Lillian herself! Learn more of her secrets and open your mind to deeper feng shui today.

Just go online to www.lilliantoomandalaezine.com and sign up today!

LILLIAN TOO's FREE NEW
Online Weekly Ezine!

Don't Miss Out! Join thousands of others who are already receiving their **FREE** updates delivered to their inbox each week.

Lillian's NEW Online FREE Weekly Ezine is only available to those who register online at www.lilliantoomandalaezine.com